SELECTED POEMS OF
GERARD MANLEY HOPKINS

D0755087

THE POETRY BOOKSHELF

General Editor: James Reeves

SELECTED POEMS OF

GERARD MANLEY HOPKINS

Edited with an Introduction
and Notes
by

JAMES REEVES

HEINEMANN

LONDON

Heinemann Educational Books Ltd

LONDON   EDINBURGH   MELBOURNE   AUCKLAND   TORONTO
SINGAPORE   HONG KONG   KUALA LUMPUR
IBADAN   NAIROBI   JOHANNESBURG
LUSAKA NEW DELHI

GERARD MANLEY HOPKINS 1844–89

ISBN 0 435 15007 3 (limp edition)
ISBN 0 435 15006 5 (cased edition)

First Published 1953
Reprinted 1954, 1956, 1958, 1959, 1961 (twice),
1964, 1966, 1967, 1970, 1972, 1974, 1975

*Hopkins' poems are published in this
selection by kind permission of the
Oxford University Press*

Published by
Heinemann Educational Books Ltd
48 Charles Street, London, W1X 8AH
Printed in Great Britain by Morrison and Gibb Ltd
London and Edinburgh

CONTENTS

PREFACE

THIS selection contains all the poems of Hopkins' maturity, together with examples of the early work and the later, unfinished pieces. The text is that of W. H. Gardner's definitive third edition of 1948. In one respect the present edition differs from previous ones: I have, after full consideration, omitted all accents marking stresses, retaining only the *grave* accents used on the final syllables of past participles (as in 'rankèd'). Some readers may deplore this; yet I believe that these stress marks have acted as a deterrent to the general appreciation of Hopkins' poems. He himself regarded them as 'offensive' and unsatisfactory, but thought them necessary at the time he wrote. Readers of modern poetry, however, are now so accustomed to accentual verse and 'the rhythm of common speech' that the marks may now be considered an unnecessary blemish. An example showing specimens of the original notation is given as an appendix.

The explanatory notes represent a compromise between brevity and adequacy. Some of the poems require a chapter of explanation. On the other hand, I have shrunk from swamping a small volume of poetry with a flood of annotation. Readers desiring a fuller treatment are directed to Dr Gardner's very thorough and exhaustive two-volume study, *Gerard Manley Hopkins: A Study of Poetic Idiosyncrasy in Relation to Poetic Tradition,* where he will find also a full bibliography of works for wider reading. I would like to acknowledge my indebtedness to these volumes, to the edition already referred to, as well as to Professor C. C. Abbott's edition of *The Letters of Gerard Manley Hopkins* in three volumes. For his indispensable help in preparing the Introduction and Notes my gratitude is due to Mr Peter Stark.   J. R.

Chalfont St Giles, 1953

Introduction

GERARD MANLEY HOPKINS
(1844–1889)

THE MAN AND THE POEMS

I

GERARD MANLEY HOPKINS, the eldest of nine children, was born
at Stratford, Essex, in June, 1844. His family was religious and
artistic. His father published a volume of verse shortly before
Gerard's birth; two of his brothers were professional artists. He
himself became proficient to more than amateur standards at
both drawing and musical composition.

From the age of ten he was at Highgate School, where he
wrote a prize poem and was awarded an exhibition in Classics
at Balliol College, Oxford. At school he showed marked
independence of spirit and intellectual precocity. One of the
masters was Richard Watson Dixon, a man eleven years his
senior, with whom he later formed a close friendship. When
he first wrote to Dixon in 1878 he described himself as having
been a conceited schoolboy. His prize poem and other early
writings show his acute sensuous perception and a capacity for
absorbing the methods of the acknowledged poets of the time—
Tennyson, Keats and, later, the Pre-Raphaelites. In another early
poem, *A Vision of the Mermaids*, written when he was eighteen,
the influence of Keats is paramount. Extreme sensuousness is felt
in every line. For all its sensuousness the poem is ascetic. At sunset
Hopkins tells us, he rowed out to a rock and saw the mermaids
gather, disport themselves, play and sing until night fell and they
disappeared beneath the sea. Yet—'Careless of me they sported'.
Such detachment would have been quite uncharacteristic in Keats.

In 1863 Hopkins went to Oxford. He showed himself, according to the testimony of Jowett, the famous Master of Balliol, a Greek scholar of uncommon promise. Far more influential than any strictly classical discipline, however, were the aesthetic doctrines of Walter Pater, his tutor. The definition of, and search for, beauty, the pursuit of art as an end in itself, might have become for Hopkins an overmastering aim, had it not been for another infinitely more persuasive influence. The religious revival within the Anglican Church begun in 1833 by John Keble, Hurrell Froude, John Henry Newman and others, and known later as the Oxford Movement, attracted growing support, and in time a section of its adherents were led to desire reunion of the national church with the Church of Rome.

The aesthetic movement under the inspiration of Ruskin and Pater was in part the outcome of a reaction by sensitive minds against Victorian materialism and ugliness. But to Hopkins, as to many others, the pursuit of beauty meant little without a specifically religious purpose. His undergraduate poems show his interest in Catholic doctrine and Pre-Raphaelite imagery.

The precise steps by which Hopkins was drawn away from the Anglican Church of his parents to follow Newman into the Church of Rome cannot be determined. The evidence of his inner life at this period and for the next dozen or so years is scanty. Many letters have been lost or destroyed. Hopkins' conversion in 1866 was decisive, yet it could not have been achieved without a struggle. The period of his uncertainty does not seem to have been prolonged, and the decision was taken at the early age of twenty-two, while he was still an undergraduate. He knew that it caused pain and shock to his parents, and he told Newman that he could not bear to re-read the letters they wrote on hearing the news.

The conversion has sometimes been written of as if it were the determining step of his life. But a more crucial one was taken two years later. On leaving Oxford with a first-class degree in

Classics, Hopkins went to teach under Newman at the Oratory School in Birmingham. In 1868 he joined the Society of Jesus. For the next nine years he studied philosophy and theology, taught Classics and underwent the spiritual discipline of a Jesuit in London, Lancashire and North Wales. In 1877 he was ordained priest.

The Society of Jesus had been founded about 1540 by Ignatius Loyola for the purpose of combating the forces of the Reformation; it was an order of priests within the Roman Church, the general laxity of which had made it unequal to the struggle against Protestantism. The Order was vowed to the most rigid standards of poverty, chastity and obedience; Ignatius had been an officer in the Spanish army, and the discipline of the Society was quasi-military; absolute devotion was exacted of all adherents. In the course of its history the Society made itself on many occasions unpopular with the Church as a whole on account of its exemplary zeal, and with the secular powers on account of its interference in politics. In various countries it was, at one time or another, proscribed. In time it became almost exclusively a missionary and educational body, and its schools were among the most admired and influential in Europe. The Society had its own hierarchy, its own saints and martyrs, above all, its tradition of unquestioning loyalty and exemplary spiritual purity.

As a Jesuit Hopkins not only vowed himself to poverty, chastity and obedience, he underwent the most exacting training in spiritual self-perfection; he gave himself, soul and body, to his Society, which undertook not only the ordering of his daily life and work, but also the regulation of his intellectual interests. During his novitiate his correspondence was censored, and throughout his life the permission of his preceptors would have to be obtained for any activity not specifically ordered.

Such a discipline Hopkins underwent freely and voluntarily. His final vows were not taken until all doubts had long been dissolved. His later expressions of dissatisfaction with the restraints put upon him are frequent; but he never wrote as if he had the slightest doubt that he belonged wholly to the Society, or as if he could conceive of his duty lying elsewhere. His attitude was that of a child fretting under the harsh but just rule of a parent whose authority, nevertheless, he never questions.

The motives and impulses which led him to sacrifice his life to the Jesuit ideal will never be fully understood. But there is a kind of temperament, as often found among Calvinists as among Catholics, which, in certain circumstances, cannot fulfil itself except through some form of self-chastisement. There was in the youthful Hopkins something priggish, something inordinately rebellious, proud and ambitious. He might have been a sensualist, and he might have been an intellectual rebel. Yet he was possessed of an unyielding moral conscience. His sensuality he punished by the vow of chastity, his pride and rebelliousness by the vow of obedience; his ambition he subjected to the discipline of personal obscurity required by the Society; and he acquired the spirit of earnestness which appeared in a more gracious form in the life and writings of Matthew Arnold.

After his ordination Hopkins lived for less than twelve years. He carried out various missions in London, Liverpool, Glasgow and other places, until his appointment to the Professorship of Greek in the Royal University of Dublin. As a student of the Classics, Hebrew, theology, philosophy, and other aesthetic and intellectual subjects, Hopkins was happy. That he was more fitted for a contemplative life than for the strenuous duties of a Jesuit priest is indicated by what he wrote on beginning the third year of his novitiate at Roehampton:

'. . . My mind is here more at peace than it has ever been and I would gladly live all my life, if it were so to be, in as great or a greater seclusion from the world and be busied only with God.'[1]

[1] Letter to Dixon, November 1881.

As a teacher he was not very successful, and as a preacher he was considered odd and ineffectual; as a parish priest he acted with unswerving devotion, but he found practical organisation irksome, and ministration in the slums of the industrial north exhausted and discouraged him. He might have been either a painter or a musician of distinction; he might have been a scholar of eminence; his correspondence is full of humour, urbanity and charm. But in pursuit of his self-imposed vocation he encountered physical ugliness and degradation which made him ill: Liverpool, Glasgow and St. Helens he found unspeakably squalid and depressing. The aesthete in him was never subdued. His earnestness made him over-conscientious in performing his duties; he became obsessed by a sense of failure and futility, and his despair seemed to envelop the whole of mankind. Holidays and visits to friends revived his spirits. A capacity for suffering involves as a rule an equally strong capacity for happiness, and Hopkins experienced frequent moments of joy and days of content. But these changes from the routine of his missions were too brief and impermanent to alter the course of his disillusion and despair.

He was not happy in Dublin. Politically he was loyal to England and he believed in the Empire. He disapproved of Gladstone's Irish policy. Above all, however, his work gave him no satisfaction. His main duties were to lecture in Classics to students for degrees, and to prepare and mark examination papers. His complaints to friends of the deadly monotony and exaction of marking are bitter and heart-felt. 'It is killing work', he wrote a year before he died, 'to examine a nation.'[1] During his first year in Dublin he was overcome by a profound melancholia, a spiritual lassitude from which there was no relief. His life-work seemed wasted and useless, his bodily strength was unequal to the demands on it; he suffered from nervous prostration which he felt might lead to madness; digestive disorder

[1] Letter to Dixon, July 1888.

and acute pain in his eyes appeared as the physical symptoms of his neurasthenia. By 1888 he had partially recovered, and his artistic impulse expressed itself in painstaking musical composition. But his health was ruined, and in June 1889 he succumbed to an attack of enteric fever.

References to his state of mind are frequent in the letters to Bridges of the last ten years of his life. Writing from Lancashire in 1880, he said:

'One is so fagged, so harried and gallied up and down. And the drunkards go on drinking—the filthy, as the scripture says, are filthy still: human nature is so inveterate. Would that I had seen the last of it.'

Even as early as 1879 this profound disquiet about 'inveterate human nature' had expressed itself in an extraordinary comment he made on sending Bridges the tender and compassionate *Bugler's First Communion*:

'I am half inclined to hope the hero of it may be killed in Afghanistan.'

From Preston in 1883 he wrote:

'I am always jaded, I cannot tell why, and my vein shows no signs of ever flowing again.'

From Dublin in 1884:

'I am, I believe, recovering from a deep fit of nervous prostration (I suppose I ought to call it): I did not know but I was dying.'

Again, a year later:

'My fits of sadness, though they do not affect my judgment, resemble madness. Change is the only relief, and that I can seldom get.'

In 1887:

'Tomorrow morning I shall have been three years in Ireland, three hard wearying wasting wasted years. . . . In those I have done God's will (in the main) and many many examination papers.'

In 1888:

> 'It seems to me I cannot always last like this: in mind or body or both I shall give way—and all I really need is a certain degree of relief and change; but I do not think that what I need I shall get in time to save me.'

But of all the confessions of desolation the most harrowing is to be found in the letter of 1st September, 1885:

> 'An old question of yours I have hitherto neglected to answer, am I thinking of writing on metre? I suppose thinking too much and doing too little. I do greatly desire to treat that subject; might perhaps get something together this year; but I can scarcely believe that on that or on anything else anything of mine will ever see the light—of publicity nor even of day. For it is widely true, the fine pleasure is not to do a thing but to feel that you could and the mortification that goes to the heart is to feel it is the power that fails you: *qui occidere nolunt Posse volunt*; it is the refusal of a thing that we like to have. So with me, if I could but get on, if I could but produce work I should not mind its being buried, silenced, and going no further; but it kills me to be time's eunuch and never to beget. After all I do not despair, things might change, anything may be; only there is no great appearance of it. Now because I have had a holiday though not strong I have some buoyancy; soon I am afraid I shall be ground down to a state like this last spring's and summer's, when my spirits were so crushed that madness seemed to be making approaches—and nobody was to blame, except myself partly for not managing myself better and contriving a change.'

Of Hopkins' inner and spiritual life we have little evidence except what can be found in, or deduced from, his poems. His most intimate records have not survived. On his death many of his letters were destroyed by the Vice-Principal of the University, and some of his papers have not yet been published. Essays and books that have been written about Hopkins during the past twenty years have varied, in the attitudes they have assumed, between the rationalistic-aesthetic on the one hand and the extreme Jesuit view on the other; the former attitude regards his adoption of the Jesuit way of life as disastrous, a mistake he ought never to have been allowed to make; the extreme Jesuit view is that his life and poetry form a harmonious whole in which everything is subordinate to the over-riding necessity of devotion to the glorification of God and the imitation of Christ. The former view is irrelevant, since we have to deal with Hopkins as he was, not as he might have been: to become a Jesuit was his choice for himself. That the renunciations and privations he endured maimed his genius and in the end killed him may be true; there can be little doubt of it. At the same time, it has to be admitted that some at least of Hopkins' finest poems are the result of this process of self-destruction. If, on the other hand, the extreme Jesuit apologist claims that there was no inner conflict, that the artist was harmoniously subordinated to the priest and the martyr, he ignores the evidence of some of Hopkins' own writings, including certain of the poems. From this point of view, the priest, the spiritual devotee of St. Ignatius and Jesus Christ is the Hopkins that matters; the poetry is an irrelevance— or at any rate, all the poetry that is not specifically doctrinal or devotional. Obviously, the two points of view cannot finally be reconciled. Hopkins himself clearly believed that he could not serve two masters—or rather, a Master and a Muse. That he himself consciously and deliberately chose to sacrifice his art and his life to the Jesuit ideal is no proof that an inner, even a sub-conscious, conflict did not take place. Art and religion were never reconciled, though he strove continually to reconcile them. Hopkins often referred to his Muse—sometimes half facetiously, it is true, but usually with a clear sense of her separate identity. He called Liverpool a 'Museless city', and writing to Bridges in 1878 he said, 'My muse turned utterly sullen in the Sheffield smoke-ridden air'; on the other hand, Wales was 'always to me a mother of Muses'. Again, defending his rhythms, he wrote, 'Some others again there are which *malignity may munch at* but the Muses love'.[1]

Writing to Dixon in 1879 about Henry Vaughan, he said: 'He was in fact converted from worldly courses by reading Herbert's poems on a sick-bed and even his muse underwent a conversion (for he had written before)'. Hopkins' muse, I believe, never underwent conversion. He never identifies her with Christ or with Mary. He was too honest to make such an easy identification. Within Hopkins the man and the Jesuit there was a poet, whom he tried first to suppress and then to convert; in this he was only partially successful. The poetic impulse was natural to him— natural and ineradicable; the will to be a Jesuit was consciously self-imposed. The martyrdom which this brought about was all the nobler, the life that ended at forty-five all the more pitiful and heroic. The poetic impulse, the creative urge, the Muse herself took terrible vengeance, reasserting herself in his last agony to wring from him the poems which are his certain assurance of immortality. It is Hopkins the poet whom we must now consider.

II

At his death Hopkins' poems had not been printed and were known to few except his friends, Bridges, Dixon and Patmore. The manuscripts were in the hands of Bridges. Between him and Hopkins there was a close literary friendship and an impassable religious barrier. Bridges disapproved of Hopkins' connection with the Jesuits. Yet he admired his contemporary's poetry: he had made use of his metrical inventions and valued and acted on his criticism. Both he and Dixon had repeatedly urged Hopkins to let them print his poems, but he had steadfastly and doggedly refused. Bridges has so often been accused of the wilful suppression of Hopkins' poems that it ought to be stated that no blame attaches to him on the evidence now available. He could not

[1] Letter to Bridges, May 1883.

have got the poems published in the 1890's if he had tried. As it was, he gradually introduced them to the public through anthologies, until he was able to print a fairly full edition in 1918. To this he attached a preface containing some ill-judged and tasteless comments; but he is not otherwise deserving of censure. The edition sold at the rate of seventy copies a year for ten years. Bridges admired, but he never understood, Hopkins' poems. His own imitations of their peculiar rhythm were thought little of by Hopkins himself, who wrote of *A Passer-by*, that celebrated anthology-piece beginning, 'Whither, O splendid ship, thy white sails crowding':

'The *Passer By* in particular reads not so much like sprung rhythm as that logaœdic dignified-doggrel one Tennyson has employed in *Maud* and since.'

Nevertheless, Bridges' efforts on his behalf were at last rewarded: the poems themselves, together with new poetic fashions, created the taste by which they could be valued truly; and from the appearance of the second edition in 1930 no post-Romantic poet has enjoyed a higher reputation. From 1930 to the present day about 46,000 copies of the collected poems have been sold (excluding sales in the U.S.A.), and the list of articles and books on Hopkins occupies five or six printed pages. Between rationalist and extreme Catholic critics an iron curtain has descended, and there seems no way of reconciling the two points of view. Meanwhile, the educated public in general has accepted Hopkins as an undisputed master, the greatest of Victorian poets, and one of the most original geniuses in the English language. His direct influence has been immense and not altogether good; it would be true to say that if Hopkins is not the founder of the modern movement in English poetry, he is its greatest forerunner. Whatever else his poetry is, it is experimental, and experimentalism has been the keynote of modern poetry. Not only are the poems themselves admired and valued as intense, urgent and passionate creations; modern readers are amazed that such poems could have been written, almost unsuspected, during the seventies and eighties of the last century, when the fashion for Tennyson, Browning and Swinburne was at its height. The very qualities which would have prevented public recognition in Hopkins' lifetime, and which called forth Bridges' censure in the preface of 1918, are those which delight readers of to-day and make the year 1875 the most important date in twentieth-century poetry.

When Hopkins joined the Society of Jesus in 1868 he burnt all his poems. The following is the account later given to Canon Dixon:

> 'What I had written I burnt before I became a Jesuit and resolved to write no more, as not belonging to my profession, unless it were by the wish of my superiors; so for seven years I wrote nothing but two or three little presentation pieces which occasion called for. But when in the winter of '75 the *Deutschland* was wrecked in the mouth of the Thames and five Franciscan nuns, exiles from Germany by the Falck laws, aboard of her were drowned, I was affected by the account and, happening to say so to my rector, he said that he wished someone would write a poem on the subject. On this hint I set to work, and though my hand was out at first, produced one. I had long had haunting my ear the echo of a new rhythm which I now realised on paper. . . . After writing this I held myself free to compose, but cannot find it in my conscience to spend time upon it; so I have done little and shall do less.'[1]

This is important because it tells us, first, that the writing of poems was against Hopkins' conscience as a Jesuit; secondly, that the necessity to write poetry forced itself upon him. Since finishing the *Deutschland* he had, however, written a number of sonnets, and even when he was writing little, he was planning larger works which never came to fruition. As he wrote to Bridges three years before his death, 'All my world is scaffolding'.

[1] Letter to Dixon, October 1878.

Yet it must be remembered that he wrote always more or less against his conscience. Perhaps he hoped that the *Deutschland* would earn him the right to compose poems as he pleased. If so, he was disappointed, for the poem, though first accepted, was afterwards rejected by the editor of the Society's journal, *The Month*. It may be that, as with other writers when composition is accompanied by a feeling of guilt, Hopkins unconsciously disguised his real motives, and concealed the true springs of his action, if not from others then from himself. All his correspondence about his poems, which was detailed and voluminous, was concerned largely with technicalities, and the same emphasis has appeared in much subsequent critical writing.

The 'new rhythm' which had been haunting his ear, and whose exploitation he offered as an explanation to Dixon of why he had composed the *Deutschland*, was the famous 'sprung rhythm'. The principle of it is that rhythm depends on stress or accent rather than on the number of feet in a line. It is, in fact, a disciplined form of free verse. Of it Hopkins wrote to Bridges: 'It is the most natural of things. It is the rhythm of common speech and of written prose, when rhythm is perceived in them'. If this was so, why, it may be asked, did Hopkins write of it elsewhere so elaborately and evolve a complicated jargon to describe its peculiarities? In the first place, to write poetry 'in the rhythm of common speech' was so revolutionary in Victorian England that technical justification must be found for it; nowadays, we are so accustomed to free verse that we can accept Hopkins' rhythm as natural and inevitable without concerning ourselves with the jargon. Moreover, as a poet Hopkins was isolated, and he valued the friendship with Bridges as an encouragement in his loneliness.

'There is a point with me in matters of any size when I must absolutely have encouragement as much as crops rain; afterwards I am independent.'[1]

[1] Letter to Bridges, May 1885.

The two were spiritually estranged, but since Bridges was a prosodist, it was natural that in their intercourse the emphasis should be on technique. Not that Hopkins' prosodic disquisitions were forced or insincere; but it cannot be doubted that when he wrote a poem it was because he had something to say and not, primarily, in order to try out a new invention. Dixon put his finger on the truth when he wrote, of sprung rhythm:

> 'Eventually, in application, I suppose it must be a matter of ear, rather than of formal rule.'[1]

This is only half the truth; it was, indeed, a matter of ear, and Hopkins had one of the most sensitive and musical ears of which we have any knowledge. He always wished that his poetry should be read with the ear. He more than once specifically states, as in a letter about *Harry Ploughman*, that it was written to be read aloud. But of course it was not a matter of ear alone. It was a matter of mind, intellect, heart, all expressing themselves by means of an appeal to the ear. The right way to read Hopkins' poems, and perhaps all great poems, is with the whole understanding geared to the sense of hearing.

Not only is the *Deutschland* a technical triumph of immense consequences, it is an intimate though obscure personal confession. It is concerned with the whole spiritual content of Hopkins' previous seven years of silence, his conversion and his dedication to the Christian life. The shipwreck was the wreck of his worldly hopes in the storm of religious revelation. The obscurity of the poem is partly the effect of the difficulty of the theme, partly the outcome of conscious or unconscious disguise. Elsewhere, Hopkins says of it that he did not wish it to be fully understood.[2]

[1] Letter from Dixon, November 1880.
[2] For a full treatment of the *Deutschland* see W. H. Gardner: *Gerard Manley Hopkins*, Vol. I. (1944), Chapter II.

After the *Deutschland* there followed a year in which Hopkins wrote little, but in 1877 there was a burst of renewed inspiration; to this year belong the sonnets expressing ecstatic wonder at the beauty of nature—*God's Grandeur, The Starlight Night, Hurrahing in Harvest, Pied Beauty, The Sea and the Skylark* and *The Windhover*. Of this last, Hopkins wrote two years later that it was the best thing he had yet done.

These are his most purely religious poems. In them he achieved a unity of poetic impulse and Christian purpose not found elsewhere. Some readers, it is true, may find the same unity in the later *Heraclitean Fire*, or even *The Blessed Virgin compared to the Air we Breathe*; but these and other doctrinal pieces are forced and intellectual by comparison, though they do not contain the specifically Catholic propaganda which mark *Andromeda, Henry Purcell* and the *Eurydice*.

The 1877 sonnets are distinguished by a simple rapture at the loveliness of the world as a manifestation of God, and by a confident, even triumphant, mastery of rhythm, diction and imagery. Except for the Dublin sonnets these are Hopkins' most uninhibited poems; his sensuous response to natural beauty is allowed full and spontaneous play. Here is 'the roll, the rise, the carol, the creation' whose loss he mourns in the final sonnet to Bridges. *The Windhover* is a perfect fusion of free inspiration and technical control; *The Starlight Night* reminds us that Hopkins' first ambition was to be a painter: it would scarcely be fanciful to call this, like *Binsey Poplars* and *Hurrahing in Harvest* poems of the French school of Impressionist painting, for they are suffused and pervaded with what seems to be less words than pure light. In *The Sea and the Skylark*, inspired by a visit to the Welsh pleasure-resort of Llandudno, the reader is almost startled by the foreboding of the theme which was later to darken Hopkins' vision, that of the brutality of civilised man amidst the pathetic and timeless beauty of nature.

Pied Beauty is widely known as an acceptable anthology piece, but it is in reality a statement of the philosophical conviction which was to colour all his work. Hopkins was an admiring student of the medieval theologian, Duns Scotus, whose theory of individuation, he believed, was based on Platonic ideas. His interest in Scotus, whom he considered the Church had unduly neglected,[1] brought him into conflict with his Jesuit preceptors,[2] since the Society favoured the teachings of Aquinas, based on Aristotle. From Scotus he derived his notion of 'inscape', in which he found the unifying principle behind all works of nature and of art.

> 'No doubt my poetry errs on the side of oddness. I hope in time to have a more balanced and Miltonic style. But as air, melody, is what strikes me most of all in music and design in painting, so design, pattern or what I am in the habit of calling 'inscape' is what I above all aim at in poetry. Now it is the virtue of design, pattern, or inscape to be distinctive and it is the vice of distinctiveness to become queer. This vice I cannot have escaped.'[3]

The importance of this statement is that it is at once the explanation and the justification of Hopkins' 'oddity'. Once we have grasped its significance, we can never again regard Hopkins as odd—though we may find other poets superficial. By 'inscape' Hopkins meant simply the outer form of all things, animate and inanimate, as it expressed their inner soul. He did not simply see things, he saw into them, and penetrated into their inmost character or being. To express his discoveries he used the utmost resources of language and imagery. Perhaps by 'inscape' he meant much the same as Roger Fry meant by the once fashionable term 'significant form'; the difference being that Fry never made it clear what his idea of form was significant *of*; Hopkins

[1] See Letter to Patmore, 3rd January 1884.
[2] According to Father Darlington, S. J., in *A Page of Irish History*.
[3] Letter to Bridges, February 1879.

had no such doubt—he was confident that the form or inscape was significant of God's presence in all things. It was God's presence which 'individuated' the constellations of the sky, the motion of bird or wind, the forms of cloud, leaf and tree. It was the sin of vandalistic man that in ravaging nature for profit he destroyed 'the inscapes of the world', as when he surrounded medieval Oxford with 'a base and brickish skirt', cut down a grove of poplars, or polluted the air with factory smoke. In *Pied Beauty*, then, Hopkins celebrated whatever was 'counter, original, spare, strange'; not only in nature but in the trades of men as well, 'their gear and tackle and trim'.

Hopkins' passion for individuality, for whatever was original, inspired his whole life and work. How far he harmonised this love of originality with the Jesuits' insistence on discipline and intellectual subordination, has created considerable divergence of opinion. But his own original genius shines out of everything he wrote in his maturity.

'The effect of studying masterpieces is to make me admire and do otherwise', was his defiant answer when Bridges urged him to model his style on the classics. Would that all Hopkins' admirers had followed his example! Nevertheless, it may be his influence that has produced the situation in contemporary poetry which caused the present Professor of Poetry at Oxford to say recently that there is no recognisable modern style in poetry. But it must be remembered that all Hopkins' deliberate originality would have been of no value if he had had nothing original to express. He has been compared to so many poets, from Aeschylus to Langland, and from Shakespeare to Whitman, that what has been hailed as originality may be, rather, a profound traditionality. Hopkins, who summed up his work in the pathetic phrase 'a lonely began', worked in almost total isolation, yet so inevitable and right do his best poems now appear that to some discerning critics it is Hopkins who is the traditionalist, and his Victorian contemporaries out of step. His own words to Bridges in 1879 are to the point:

> 'It seems to me that the poetical language of an age shd. be the current language heightened, to any degree heightened and unlike itself, but not (I mean normally: passing freaks and graces are another thing) an obsolete one. This is Shakespeare's and Milton's practice and the want of it will be fatal to Tennyson's Idylls and plays, to Swinburne, and perhaps to Morris.'

Those who deplore Hopkins' adherence to the Jesuit Order should reflect that the same unflinching hardness of purpose showed itself in his determination to follow his own light in poetry. He could hardly have done this if his work had been subject to all the winds of criticism and fashion which blew upon the published poems of his contemporaries. Dr Leavis is right when he says:

> '. . . Hopkins' genius was as much a matter of rare character, intelligence and sincerity as of technical skill: indeed, in his great poetry the distinction disappears; the technical triumph is a triumph of spirit.'[1]

The sonnets of 1877 were followed by another year barren except for *The Loss of the Eurydice*. This also was offered to the Editor of *The Month* and rejected. In 1879 and 1880 there was another poetic outburst, in which humanity rather than nature is the theme. *The Bugler's First Communion, The Candle Indoors, The Handsome Heart, Felix Randal*, and *Brothers* all deal directly with Hopkins' work as a priest in the world of ordinary men. These poems have not the spontaneous joy of the earlier sonnets, nor their richness of imagery and suggestion; yet throughout there is a note of tenderness and pity not found in the work of any other period. If *Felix Randal* is not the most rapturous or the most profound of Hopkins' poems, it is the most compassionate and touching. Pity, again, for frail mortality is the theme of

[1] *New Bearings in English Poetry*, Chapter V.

Spring and Fall, written, Hopkins told Bridges, on an imaginary incident.

Yet the mood did not last. Despair and disillusion were already checking the springs of humanity in Hopkins. Revived concern with this theme is shown in two poems written near the time of his death, *Tom's Garland*, a poem on the town labourer, and *Harry Ploughman*, a companion poem. In the latter something of the tone and mood of the early sonnets on nature is recaptured.

The years 1881 to 1884 reveal an almost complete failure of inspiration. Hopkins wrote, from a sense of duty, a few occasional pieces devoted to the Catholic cause; but in these he took little satisfaction. 1884 is a year of silence, in which spiritual languor, despair over his work, the sense of frustration and failure, and the desolation which came from a feeling of being deserted by God himself, broke over him in an annihilating wave. From this he emerged to make his last great poetic utterance. The series of sonnets which begins with *Spelt from Sibyl's Leaves* and ends with that *To R.B.* enclosed with his last letter to his friend is among the unquestionably great poems of all time. There is the same daring innovation in language, the same earnestness and originality that had distinguished his earlier work, but there is a new and sombre majesty of tone, an even greater intensity, a concentrated passion of utterance in which a profoundly sensitive and civilised spirit raises itself from its death-bed to make a last attempt at regeneration through poetry. These 'terrible sonnets', as they have been called, are the uncensored expression of Hopkins' naked soul. Sending five of them to Bridges in 1885 he wrote:

'Four of these came like inspirations unbidden and against my will. And in the life I lead now, which is one of a continually jaded and harassed mind, if in any leisure I try to do anything I make no way—nor with my work, alas! but so it must be.'

It is probable that the four referred to are *Carrion Comfort*,

No worst, there is none, *I wake and feel the fell of dark*, and *To seem the stranger lies my lot*. The theme of these sonnets and of the two written in the last few months of his life—*Thou art indeed just, Lord*, and *To R.B.*—is threefold: the darkness that has enveloped the whole of creation; the desertion of God and the failure of inspiration, the fate that has made him 'time's eunuch'. The images are those of darkness, horror and sterility. Nothing in all English poetry is so powerful, outside *Macbeth*. The rhythm is the direct expression of a crushed and bleeding desperation. *Carrion Comfort* he described as being 'written in blood'.

Yet this mood must have been at least partially overcome in the very act of writing the poems. A man swallowed up in the suffocating folds of neurasthenia does not write poems like these, or any poems. Hopkins had faced the alternative of madness or death. There is no evidence that he wavered in his devotion to the Jesuit ideal; but it is clear that he turned to poetry above everything else for the recovery from, and the justification of, his sufferings. In poetry he triumphed over the utter disintegration which threatened his being. In *Patience, hard thing!* and *My own heart let me more have pity on* he expressed Christian resignation yet his honesty allowed of no final consolation for his sense of frustration. The last two sonnets return to the theme of sterility. *Thou art indeed just, Lord* is a hurt and defiant protest against the God who seemed to have favoured sinners more than his dedicated servant. In *To R.B.* he makes his final admission of total failure.

The 'ruins of wrecked past purpose' of which Hopkins wrote in *Patience, hard thing!* were no mere fantasies. For years he had suffered from his inability to finish various ambitious works begun and laid aside. *The Leaden Echo and the Golden Echo*, for instance, is a chorus from the poetic tragedy *St Winefred's Well* of which he wrote only a few fragments and which he longed to accomplish. Other projects in both poetry and music are discussed freely in the letters to his friends. We may try to find in

Hopkins' work the expression of his whole personality, but to him it was little more than a collection of fragments, experiments, spasmodic pieces produced because he could not help producing something, even though it was not the greater works he planned. As early as 1879 he had written to Bridges:

'When I say that I do not mean to publish I speak the truth. I have taken and mean to take no step to do so beyond the attempt I made to print my two wrecks in the *Month*. If some-one in authority knew of my having some poems printable and suggested my doing it I shd. not refuse. I should be partly though not altogether glad. But that is very unlikely. All therefore that I think of doing is to keep my verses together in one place—at present, I have not even correct copies—, that, if anyone shd. like, they might be published after my death. And that again is unlikely as well as remote. . . . I cannot in conscience spend time on poetry, neither have I the inducements and inspirations that make others compose. Feeling, love in particular, is the great moving power and spring of verse and the only person that I am in love with seldom, especially now, stirs my heart sensibly and when he does I cannot always "make capital" of it, it would be a sacrilege to do so.'

Hopkins' attitude towards fame and reputation was perfectly clear.

'By the bye, I say it deliberately and before God, I would have you and Canon Dixon and all true poets remember that fame, the being known, though in itself one of the most dangerous things to man, is nevertheless the true and appointed air, element, and setting of genius and its works. . . . We must then try to be known, aim at it, take means to it.'[1]

Yet he knew that such fame was not, and could never be his during his lifetime. His priestly vows involved certain definite hardships and privations which he accepted as part of his sacrifice to God. But to a poet of genius and originality the deliberate renunciation of fame must, despite his words to the

[1] Letter to Bridges, October 1886.

contrary, have been a hardship. He wrote of his own poems always with the perfect modesty of a man who knows his own worth; he knew in his heart, though he never said as much, that he was a better poet than any that were popular in his time. He was always anxious for the reputation and success of his friend Bridges: in a sense they were a substitute for the fame he himself could never have. Nor did he ever speak mawkishly about a possible posthumous fame. Why, then, did he write poems, and why did he project even more?

> 'It always seems to me', he wrote to Bridges in 1884, 'that poetry is unprofessional, but that is what I have said to myself, not others to me. No doubt if I kept producing I should have to ask myself what I meant to do with it all; but I have long been at a standstill, and so the things lie.'

Everything he did as a Jesuit was done, according to the official formula, 'ad majorem Dei gloriam'. So it might be of his presentation pieces, and even of such successes as *The Windhover*. But there was much that Hopkins wrote—had to write—which he could never reconcile with the avowed aims of the Society, however ingeniously some of his successors have laboured to do so. His life was dedicated to God, but many of his poems he must have dedicated, in his heart, to the poetic spirit that had been born in him, to his Muse, or to posterity. There is nowhere in his writings a gleam of confidence that his genius will ever be recognised. Yet by one of those paradoxes in which, as a Christian and a Jesuit, he must have delighted, it is that fearless devotion to the poetic ideal in facing what he thought to be his failure and annihilation that has earned his poetry its posthumous reward. The poems which have earned him our highest regard are not those he would have written if he had believed in any such reward for himself after death. That this was no accident but an expression of the 'divinity that shapes our ends', Hopkins himself would have had no doubt.

EARLY POEMS

Heaven-Haven

A nun takes the veil

I have desired to go
    Where springs not fail,
To fields where flies no sharp and sided hail
    And a few lilies blow.

And I have asked to be
    Where no storms come,
Where the green swell is in the havens dumb
    And out of the swing of the sea.

The Habit of Perfection

Elected Silence, sing to me
And beat upon my whorlèd ear,
Pipe me to pastures still and be
The music that I care to hear.

Shape nothing, lips; be lovely-dumb:
It is the shut, the curfew sent
From there where all surrenders come
Which only makes you eloquent.

Be shellèd, eyes, with double dark
And find the uncreated light:
This ruck and reel which you remark
Coils, keeps, and teases simple sight.

Palate, the hutch of tasty lust,
Desire not to be rinsed with wine:
The can must be so sweet, the crust
So fresh that come in fasts divine!

Nostrils, your careless breath that spend
Upon the stir and keep of pride,
What relish shall the censers send
Along the sanctuary side!

O feel-of-primrose hands, O feet
That want the yield of plushy sward,
But you shall walk the golden street
And you unhouse and house the Lord.

And' Poverty, be thou the bride
And now the marriage feast begun,
And lily-coloured clothes provide
Your spouse not laboured-at nor spun.

POEMS, 1876–89

The Wreck of the Deutschland

To the
happy memory of five Franciscan Nuns
exiles by the Falk Laws
drowned between midnight and morning of
Dec. 7th 1875

PART THE FIRST

1

Thou mastering me
God! giver of breath and bread;
World's strand, sway of the sea;
Lord of living and dead;
Thou hast bound bones and veins in me, fastened me flesh,
And after it almost unmade, what with dread,
Thy doing: and dost thou touch me afresh?
Over again I feel thy finger and find thee.

2

I did say yes
O at lightning and lashed rod;
Thou heardst me truer than tongue confess
Thy terror, O Christ, O God;
Thou knowest the walls, altar and hour and night:
The swoon of a heart that the sweep and the hurl of thee
trod
Hard down with a horror of height:
And the midriff astrain with leaning of, laced with fire of stress.

3

3

The frown of his face
Before me, the hurtle of hell
Behind, where, where was a, where was a place?
I whirled out wings that spell
And fled with a fling of the heart to the heart of the Host.
My heart, but you were dovewinged, I can tell,
Carrier-witted, I am bold to boast,
To flash from the flame to the flame then, tower from the grace
to the grace.

4

I am soft sift
In an hourglass—at the wall
Fast, but mined with a motion, a drift,
And it crowds and it combs to the fall;
I steady as a water in a well, to a poise, to a pane,
But roped with, always, all the way down from the tall
Fells or flanks of the voel, a vein
Of the gospel proffer, a pressure, a principle, Christ's gift.

5

I kiss my hand
To the stars, lovely-asunder
Starlight, wafting him out of it; and
Glow, glory in thunder;
Kiss my hand to the dappled-with-damson west:
Since, tho' he is under the world's splendour and wonder,
His mystery must be instressed, stressed;
For I greet him the days I meet him, and bless when I understand.

6

Not out of his bliss
Springs the stress felt
Nor first from heaven (and few know this)
Swings the stroke dealt—

Stroke and a stress that stars and storms deliver,
That guilt is hushed by, hearts are flushed by and melt—
    But it rides time like riding a river
(And here the faithful waver, the faithless fable and miss).

7

    It dates from day
    Of his going in Galilee;
Warm-laid grave of a womb-life grey;
    Manger, maiden's knee;
The dense and the driven Passion, and frightful sweat;
Thence the discharge of it, there its swelling to be,
    Though felt before, though in high flood yet—
What none would have known of it, only the heart, being hard
    at bay,

8

    Is out with it! Oh,
    We lash with the best or worst
Word last! How a lush-kept plush-capped sloe
    Will, mouthed to flesh-burst,
Gush!—flush the man, the being with it, sour or sweet,
Brim, in a flash, full!—Hither then, last or first,
    To hero of Calvary, Christ's feet—
Never ask if meaning it, wanting it, warned of it—men go.

9

    Be adored among men,
    God, three-numberèd form;
Wring thy rebel, dogged in den,
    Man's malice, with wrecking and storm.
Beyond saying sweet, past telling of tongue,
Thou art lightning and love, I found it, a winter and warm:
    Father and fondler of heart thou hast wrung:
Hast thy dark descending and most art merciful then.

5

With an anvil-ding
And with fire in him forge thy will
Or rather, rather then, stealing as Spring
Through him, melt him but master him still:
Whether at once, as once at a crash Paul,
Or as Austin, a lingering-out sweet skill,
Make mercy in all of us, out of us all
Mastery, but be adored, but be adored King.

PART THE SECOND

11

'Some find me a sword; some
The flange and the rail; flame,
Fang, or flood' goes Death on drum,
And storms bugle his fame.
But we dream we are rooted in earth—Dust!
Flesh falls within sight of us, we, though our flower the
same,
Wave with the meadow, forget that there must
The sour scythe cringe, and the blear share come.

12

On Saturday sailed from Bremen,
American-outward-bound,
Take settler and seamen, tell men with women,
Two hundred souls in the round—
O Father, not under thy feathers nor ever as guessing
The goal was a shoal, of a fourth the doom to be drowned;
Yet did the dark side of the bay of thy blessing
Not vault them, the millions of rounds of thy mercy not reeve
even them in?

Into the snows she sweeps,
  Hurling the haven behind,
The Deutschland, on Sunday; and so the sky keeps,
  For the infinite air is unkind,
And the sea flint-flake, black-backed in the regular blow.
Sitting Eastnortheast, in cursed quarter, the wind;
  Wiry and white-fiery and whirlwind-swivellèd snow
Spins to the widow-making unchilding unfathering deeps.

14

She drove in the dark to leeward,
  She struck—not a reef or a rock
But the combs of a smother of sand: night drew her
  Dead to the Kentish Knock;
And she beat the bank down with her bows and the ride of
  her keel:
The breakers rolled on her beam with ruinous shock:
  And canvas and compass, the whorl and the wheel
Idle for ever to waft her or wind her with, these she endured.

Hope had grown grey hairs,
  Hope had mourning on,
Trenched with tears, carved with cares,
  Hope was twelve hours gone;
And frightful a nightfall folded rueful a day
Nor rescue, only rocket and lightship, shone,
  And lives at last were washing away:
To the shrouds they took,—they shook in the hurling and
  horrible airs.

One stirred from the rigging to save
The wild woman-kind below,
With a rope's end round the man, handy and brave—
He was pitched to his death at a blow,
For all his dreadnought breast and braids of thew:
They could tell him for hours, dandled the to and fro
Through the cobbled foam-fleece, what could he do
With the burl of the fountains of air, buck and the flood of the
wave?

17

They fought with God's cold—
And they could not and fell to the deck
(Crushed them) or water (and drowned them) or
rolled
With the sea-romp over the wreck.
Night roared, with the heart-break hearing a heart-broke
rabble,
The woman's wailing, the crying of child without check—
Till a lioness arose breasting the babble,
A prophetess towered in the tumult, a virginal tongue told.

Ah, touched in your bower of bone
Are you! turned for an exquisite smart,
Have you! make words break from me here all alone,
Do you!—mother of being in me, heart.
O unteachably after evil, but uttering truth,
Why, tears! is it? tears; such a melting, a madrigal start!
Never-eldering revel and river of youth,
What can it be, this glee? the good you have there of your
own?

Sister, a sister calling
A master, her master and mine!—
And the inboard seas run swirling and hawling;
The rash smart sloggering brine
Blinds her; but she that weather sees one thing, one;
Has one fetch in her: she rears herself to divine
Ears, and the call of the tall nun
To the men in the tops and the tackle rode over the storm's
brawling.

She was first of a five and came
Of a coifèd sisterhood.
(O Deutschland, double a desperate name!
O world wide of its good!
But Gertrude, lily, and Luther, are two of a town,
Christ's lily and beast of the waste wood:
From life's dawn it is drawn down,
Abel is Cain's brother and breasts they have sucked the
same.)

Loathed for a love men knew in them,
Banned by the land of their birth,
Rhine refused them. Thames would ruin them;
Surf, snow, river and earth
Gnashed: but thou art above, thou Orion of light;
Thy unchancelling poising palms were weighing the worth,
Thou martyr-master: in thy sight
Storm flakes were scroll-leaved flowers, lily showers—sweet
heaven was astrew in them.

Five! the finding and sake
And cipher of suffering Christ.
Mark, the mark is of man's make
And the word of it Sacrificed.
But he scores it in scarlet himself on his own bespoken,
Before-time-taken, dearest prizèd and priced—
Stigma, signal, cinquefoil token
For lettering of the lamb's fleece, ruddying of the rose-flake.

Joy fall to thee, father Francis,
Drawn to the Life that died;
With the gnarls of the nails in thee, niche of the lance,
    his
Lovescape crucified
And seal of his seraph-arrival! and these thy daughters
And five-livèd and leavèd favour and pride,
Are sisterly sealed in wild waters,
To bathe in his fall-gold mercies, to breathe in his all-fire
glances.

Away in the loveable west,
On a pastoral forehead of Wales,
I was under a roof here, I was at rest,
And they the prey of the gales;
She to the black-about air, to the breaker, the thickly
Falling flakes, to the throng that catches and quails
Was calling 'O Christ, Christ, come quickly':
The cross to her she calls Christ to her, christens her wild-worst
Best.

The majesty! what did she mean?
Breathe, arch and original Breath.
Is it love in her of the being as her lover had been?
Breathe, body of lovely Death.
They were else-minded then, altogether, the men
Woke thee with a *we are perishing* in the weather of Gennesareth.
Or is it that she cried for the crown then,
The keener to come at the comfort for feeling the combating keen?

For how to the heart's cheering
The down-dugged ground-hugged grey
Hovers off, the jay-blue heavens appearing
Of pied and peeled May!
Blue-beating and hoary-glow height; or night, still higher,
With belled fire and the moth-soft Milky Way,
What by your measure is the heaven of desire,
The treasure never eyesight got, nor was ever guessed what for the hearing?

No, but it was not these.
The jading and jar of the cart,
Time's tasking, it is fathers that asking for ease
Of the sodden-with-its-sorrowing heart,
Not danger, electrical horror; then further it finds
The appealing of the Passion is tenderer in prayer apart:
Other, I gather, in measure her mind's
Burden, in wind's burly and beat of endragonèd seas.

28

But how shall I . . . make me room there:
Reach me a . . . Fancy, come faster—
Strike you the sight of it? look at it loom there,
Thing that she . . . there then! the Master,
Ipse, the only one, Christ, King, Head:
He was to cure the extremity where he had cast her;
Do, deal, lord it with living and dead;
Let him ride, her pride, in his triumph, despatch and have done
with his doom there.

29

Ah! there was a heart right
There was single eye!
Read the unshapeable shock night
And knew the who and the why;
Wording it how but by him that present and past,
Heaven and earth are word of, worded by?—
The Simon Peter of a soul! to the blast
Tarpeian-fast, but a blown beacon of light.

30

Jesu, heart's light,
Jesu, maid's son,
What was the feast followed the night
Thou hadst glory of this nun?—
Feast of the one woman without stain.
For so conceivèd, so to conceive thee is done;
But here was heart-throe, birth of a brain,
Word, that heard and kept thee and uttered thee outright.

Well, she has thee for the pain, for the
Patience; but pity of the rest of them!
Heart, go and bleed at a bitterer vein for the
Comfortless unconfessed of them—
No not uncomforted: lovely-felicitous Providence
Finger of a tender of, O of a feathery delicacy, the breast
of the
Maiden could obey so, be a bell to, ring of it, and
Startle the poor sheep back! is the shipwrack then a harvest,
does tempest carry the grain for thee?

I admire thee, master of the tides,
Of the Yore-flood, of the year's fall;
The recurb and the recovery of the gulf's sides,
The girth of it and the wharf of it and the wall;
Stanching, quenching ocean of a motionable mind;
Ground of being, and granite of it; past all
Grasp God, throned behind
Death with a sovereignty that heeds but hides, bodes but abides;

With a mercy that outrides
The all of water, an ark
For the listener; for the lingerer with a love glides
Lower than death and the dark;
A vein for the visiting of the past-prayer, pent in prison,
The-last-breath penitent spirits—the uttermost mark
Our passion-plungèd giant risen,
The Christ of the Father compassionate, fetched in the storm
of his strides.

34

Now burn, new born to the world,
Doubled-naturèd name,
The heaven-flung, heart-fleshed, maiden-furled
Miracle-in-Mary-of-flame,
Mid-numbered He in three of the thunder-throne!
Not a dooms-day dazzle in his coming nor dark as he came;
Kind, but royally reclaiming his own;
A released shower, let flash to the shire, not a lightning of fire
hard-hurled.

35

Dame, at our door
Drowned, and among our shoals,
Remember us in the roads, the heaven-haven of the
Reward:
Our King back, oh, upon English souls!
Let him easter in us, be a dayspring to the dimness of us,
be a crimson-cresseted east,
More brightening her, rare-dear Britain, as his reign rolls,
Pride, rose, prince, hero of us, high-priest,
Our hearts' charity's hearth's fire, our thoughts' chivalry's
throng's Lord.

Penmaen Pool

For the Visitors' Book at the Inn

Who long for rest, who look for pleasure
Away from counter, court, or school
O where live well your lease of leisure
But here at, here at Penmaen Pool?

You'll dare the Alp? you'll dart the skiff?—
Each sport has here its tackle and tool:
Come, plant the staff by Cadair cliff;
Come, swing the sculls on Penmaen Pool.

What's yonder?—Grizzled Dyphwys dim:
The triple-hummocked Giant's stool,
Hoar messmate, hobs and nobs with him
To halve the bowl of Penmaen Pool.

And all the landscape under survey,
At tranquil turns, by nature's rule,
Rides repeated topsyturvy
In frank, in fairy Penmaen Pool.

And Charles's Wain, the wondrous seven,
And sheep-flock clouds like worlds of wool,
For all they shine so, high in heaven,
Shew brighter shaken in Penmaen Pool.

The Mawddach, how she trips! though throttled
If floodtide teeming thrills her full,
And mazy sands all water-wattled
Waylay her at ebb, past Penmaen Pool.

But what's to see in stormy weather,
When grey showers gather and gusts are cool?—
Why, raindrop-roundels looped together
That lace the face of Penmaen Pool.

Then even in weariest wintry hour
Of New Year's month or surly Yule
Furred snows, charged tuft above tuft, tower
From darksome darksome Penmaen Pool.

And ever, if bound here hardest home,
You've parlour-pastime left and (who'll
Not honour it?) ale like goldy foam
That frocks an oar in Penmaen Pool.

Then come who pine for peace or pleasure
Away from counter, court, or school,
Spend here your measure of time and treasure
And taste the treats of Penmaen Pool.

The Silver Jubilee

To James First Bishop of Shrewsbury on the
25th Year of his Episcopate July 28, 1876

1

Though no high-hung bells or din
Of braggart bugles cry it in—
   What is sound? Nature's round
Makes the Silver Jubilee.

2

Five and twenty years have run
Since sacred fountains to the sun
   Sprang, that but now were shut,
Showering Silver Jubilee.

3

Feasts, when we shall fall asleep,
Shrewsbury may see others keep;
   None but you this her true,
This her Silver Jubilee.

4

Not today we need lament
Your wealth of life is some way spent:
   Toil has shed round your head
Silver but for Jubilee.

5

Then for her whose velvet vales
Should have pealed with welcome, Wales,
   Let the chime of a rhyme
Utter Silver Jubilee.

God's Grandeur

The world is charged with the grandeur of God.
   It will flame out, like shining from shook foil;
   It gathers to a greatness, like the ooze of oil
Crushed. Why do men then now not reck his rod?
Generations have trod, have trod, have trod;
   And all is seared with trade; bleared, smeared with toil;
   And wears man's smudge and shares man's smell: the soil
Is bare now, nor can foot feel, being shod.

And for all this, nature is never spent;
   There lives the dearest freshness deep down things;
And though the last lights off the black West went
   Oh, morning, at the brown brink eastward, springs—
Because the Holy Ghost over the bent
   World broods with warm breast and with ah! bright wings.

The Starlight Night

Look at the stars! look, look up at the skies!
  O look at all the fire-folk sitting in the air!
  The bright boroughs, the circle-citadels there!
Down in dim woods the diamond delves! the elves'-eyes!
The grey lawns cold where gold, where quickgold lies!
  Wind-beat whitebeam! airy abeles set on a flare!
  Flake-doves sent floating forth at a farmyard scare!—
Ah well! it is all a purchase, all is a prize.

Buy then! bid then!—What?—Prayer, patience, alms, vows.
Look, look: a May-mess, like on orchard boughs!
  Look! March-bloom, like on mealed-with-yellow sallows!
These are indeed the barn; withindoors house
The shocks. This piece-bright paling shuts the spouse
  Christ home, Christ and his mother and all his hallows.

Spring

Nothing is so beautiful as spring—
  When weeds, in wheels, shoot long and lovely and lush;
  Thrush's eggs look little low heavens, and thrush
Through the echoing timber does so rinse and wring
The ear, it strikes like lightnings to hear him sing;
  The glassy peartree leaves and blooms, they brush
  The descending blue; that blue is all in a rush
With richness; the racing lambs too have fair their fling.

What is all this juice and all this joy?
  A strain of the earth's sweet being in the beginning
In Eden garden.—Have, get, before it cloy,
  Before it cloud, Christ, lord, and sour with sinning,
Innocent mind and Mayday in girl and boy,
  Most, O maid's child, thy choice and worthy the winning.

The Lantern out of Doors

Sometimes a lantern moves along the night,
  That interests our eyes. And who goes there?
  I think; where from and bound, I wonder, where,
With, all down darkness wide, his wading light?

Men go by me whom either beauty bright
  In mould or mind or what not else makes rare:
  They rain against our much-thick and marsh air
Rich beams, till death or distance buys them quite.

Death or distance soon consumes them: wind
  What most I may eye after, be in at the end
I cannot, and out of sight is out of mind.

Christ minds; Christ's interest, what to avow or amend
  There, eyes them, heart wants, care haunts, foot follows kind,
Their ransom, their rescue, and first, fast, last friend.

The Sea and the Skylark

On ear and ear two noises too old to end
  Trench—right, the tide that ramps against the shore;
  With a flood or a fall, low lull-off or all roar,
Frequenting there while moon shall wear and wend.

Left hand, off land, I hear the lark ascend,
  His rash-fresh re-winded new-skeinèd score
  In crisps of curl off wild winch whirl, and pour
And pelt music, till none's to spill nor spend.

How these two shame this shallow and frail town!
  How ring right out our sordid turbid time,
Being pure! We, life's pride and cared-for crown,

  Have lost that cheer and charm of earth's past prime:
Our make and making break, are breaking, down
  To man's last dust, drain fast towards man's first slime.

The Windhover

To Christ our Lord

I caught this morning morning's minion, king-
    dom of daylight's dauphin, dapple-dawn-drawn Falcon, in
      his riding
Of the rolling level underneath him steady air, and striding
High there, how he rung upon the rein of a wimpling wing
In his ecstasy! then off, off forth on swing,
    As a skate's heel sweeps smooth on a bow-bend: the hurl and
      gliding
    Rebuffed the big wind. My heart in hiding
Stirred for a bird,—the achieve of, the mastery of the thing!

Brute beauty and valour and act, oh, air, pride, plume, here
    Buckle ! AND the fire that breaks from thee then, a billion
Times told lovelier, more dangerous, O my chevalier!

    No wonder of it: sheer plod makes plough down sillion
Shine, and blue-bleak embers, ah my dear,
    Fall, gall themselves, and gash gold-vermilion.

Pied Beauty

Glory be to God for dappled things—
    For skies of couple-colour as a brinded cow;
        For rose-moles all in stipple upon trout that swim;
Fresh-firecoal chestnut-falls; finches' wings;
    Landscape plotted and pieced—fold, fallow, and plough;
        And all trades, their gear and tackle and trim.

All things counter, original, spare, strange;
    Whatever is fickle, freckled (who knows how?)
        With swift, slow; sweet, sour; adazzle, dim:
He fathers-forth whose beauty is past change:
           Praise him.

Hurrahing in Harvest

Summer ends now; now, barbarous in beauty, the stooks arise
   Around; up above, what wind-walks! what lovely behaviour
   Of silk-sack clouds! has wilder, wilful-wavier
Meal-drift moulded ever and melted across skies?

I walk, I lift up, I lift up heart, eyes,
   Down all that glory in the heavens to glean our Saviour;
   And, eyes, heart, what looks, what lips yet gave you a
Rapturous love's greeting of realer, of rounder replies?

And the azurous hung hills are his world-wielding shoulder
   Majestic—as a stallion stalwart, very-violet-sweet!—
These things, these things were here and but the beholder
   Wanting; which two when they once meet,
The heart rears wings bold and bolder
   And hurls for him, O half hurls earth for him off under
      his feet.

The Caged Skylark

As a dare-gale skylark scanted in a dull cage
    Man's mounting spirit in his bone-house, mean house,
        dwells—
    That bird beyond the remembering his free fells;
This in drudgery, day-labouring-out life's age.

Though aloft on turf or perch or poor low stage,
    Both sing sometimes the sweetest, sweetest spells,
    Yet both droop deadly sometimes in their cells
Or wring their barriers in bursts of fear or rage.

Not that the sweet-fowl, song-fowl, needs no rest—
Why, hear him, hear him babble and drop down to his nest,
    But his own nest, wild nest, no prison.

Man's spirit will be flesh-bound when found at best,
But uncumbered: meadow-down is not distressed
    For a rainbow footing it nor he for his bones risen.

In the Valley of the Elwy

I remember a house where all were good
   To me, God knows, deserving no such thing:
   Comforting smell breathed at very entering,
Fetched fresh, as I suppose, off some sweet wood.
That cordial air made those kind people a hood
   All over, as a bevy of eggs the mothering wing
   Will, or mild nights the new morsels of spring:
Why, it seemed of course; seemed of right it should.

Lovely the woods, waters, meadows, combes, vales,
All the air things wear that build this world of Wales;
   Only the inmate does not correspond:
God, lover of souls, swaying considerate scales,
Complete thy creature dear O where it fails,
   Being mighty a master, being a father and fond.

The Loss of the Eurydice

Foundered March 24, 1878

1

The Eurydice—it concerned thee, O Lord:
Three hundred souls, O alas! on board,
    Some asleep unawakened, all un-
warned, eleven fathoms fallen

2

Where she foundered! One stroke
Felled and furled them, the hearts of oak!
    And flockbells off the aerial
Downs' forefalls beat to the burial.

3

For did she pride her, freighted fully, on
Bounden bales or a hoard of bullion?—
    Precious passing measure,
Lads and men her lade and treasure.

4

She had come from a cruise, training seamen—
Men, boldboys soon to be men:
    Must it, worst weather,
Blast bole and bloom together?

5

No Atlantic squall overwrought her
Or rearing billow of the Biscay water:
    Home was hard at hand
And the blow bore from land.

6

And you were a liar, O blue March day.
Bright sun lanced fire in the heavenly bay;
    But what black Boreas wrecked her? he
Came equipped, deadly-electric,

7

A beetling baldbright cloud thorough England
Riding: there did storms not mingle? and
    Hailropes hustle and grind their
Heavengravel? wolfsnow, worlds of it, wind there?

8

Now Carisbrook keep goes under in gloom;
Now it overvaults Appledurcombe;
    Now near by Ventnor town
It hurls, hurls off Boniface Down.

9

Too proud, too proud, what a press she bore!
Royal, and all her royals wore.
    Sharp with her, shorten sail!
Too late; lost; gone with the gale.

10

This was that fell capsize,
As half she had righted and hoped to rise
    Death teeming in by her portholes
Raced down decks, round messes of mortals.

11

Then a lurch forward, frigate and men;
'All hands for themselves' the cry ran then;
    But she who had housed them thither
Was around them, bound them or wound them with her.

12

Marcus Hare, high her captain,
Kept to her—care-drowned and wrapped in
    Cheer's death, would follow
His charge through the champ-white water-in-a-wallow.

13

All under Channel to bury in a beach her
Cheeks: Right, rude of feature,
    He thought he heard say
'Her commander! and thou too, and thou this way.'

14

It is even seen, time's something server,
In mankind's medley a duty-swerver,
    At downright 'No or yes?'
Doffs all, drives full for righteousness.

15

Sydney Fletcher, Bristol-bred,
(Low lie his mates now on watery bed)
    Takes to the sea and snows
As sheer down the ship goes.

16

Now her afterdraught gullies him too down;
Now he wrings for breath with the deathgush brown;
    Till a lifebelt and God's will
Lend him a lift from the sea-swill.

17

Now he shoots short up to the round air;
Now he gasps, now he gazes everywhere;
    But his eye no cliff, no coast or
Mark makes in the rivelling snowstorm.

Him, after an hour of wintry waves,
A schooner sights, with another, and saves,
    And he boards her in Oh! such joy
He has lost count what came next, poor boy.—

They say who saw one sea-corpse cold
He was all of lovely manly mould,
    Every inch a tar,
Of the best we boast our sailors are.

Look, foot to forelock, how all things suit! he
Is strung by duty, is strained to beauty,
    And brown-as-dawning-skinned
With brine and shine and whirling wind.

O his nimble finger, his gnarled grip!
Leagues, leagues of seamanship
    Slumber in these forsaken
Bones, this sinew, and will not waken.

He was but one like thousands more,
Day and night I deplore
    My people and born own nation,
Fast foundering own generation.

I might let bygones be—our curse
Of ruinous shrine no hand or, worse,
    Robbery's hand is busy to
Dress, hoar-hallowèd shrines unvisited;

24

Only the breathing temple and fleet
Life, this wildworth blown so sweet,
      These daredeaths, ay this crew, in
Unchrist, all rolled in ruin—

25

Deeply surely I need to deplore it,
Wondering why my master bore it,
      The riving off that race
So at home, time was, to his truth and grace

26

That a starlight-wender of ours would say
The marvellous Milk was Walsingham Way
      And one—but let be, let be:
More, more than was will yet be.—

27

O well wept, mother have lost son;
Wept, wife; wept, sweetheart would be one:
      Though grief yield them no good
Yet shed what tears sad truelove should.

28

But to Christ lord of thunder
Crouch; lay knee by earth low under:
      'Holiest, loveliest, bravest,
Save my hero, O Hero savest.

29

And the prayer thou hearst me making
Have, at the awful overtaking,
      Heard; have heard and granted
Grace that day grace was wanted.'

30

Not that hell knows redeeming,
But for souls sunk in seeming
    Fresh, till doomfire burn all,
Prayer shall fetch pity eternal

33

The May Magnificat

May is Mary's month, and I
Muse at that and wonder why:
    Her feasts follow reason,
    Dated due to season—

Candlemas, Lady Day;
But the Lady Month, May,
    Why fasten that upon her,
    With a feasting in her honour?

Is it only its being brighter
Than the most are must delight her?
    Is it opportunest
    And flowers finds soonest?

Ask of her, the mighty mother:
Her reply puts this other
    Question: What is Spring?—
    Growth in every thing—

Flesh and fleece, fur and feather,
Grass and greenworld all together;
    Star-eyed strawberry-breasted
    Throstle above her nested

Cluster of bugle blue eggs thin
Forms and warms the life within;
    And bird and blossom swell
    In sod or sheath or shell.

All things rising, all things sizing
Mary sees, sympathising
    With that world of good,
    Nature's motherhood.

Their magnifying of each its kind
With delight calls to mind
    How she did in her stored
    Magnify the Lord.

Well but there was more than this:
Spring's universal bliss
    Much, had much to say
    To offering Mary May.

When drop-of-blood-and-foam-dapple
Bloom lights the orchard-apple
    And thicket and thorp are merry
    With silver-surfèd cherry

And azuring-over greybell makes
Wood banks and brakes wash wet like lake.
    And magic cuckoocall
    Caps, clears, and clinches all—

This ecstasy all through mothering earth
Tells Mary her mirth till Christ's birth
    To remember and exultation
    In God who was her salvation.

Binsey Poplars

felled 1879

My aspens dear, whose airy cages quelled,
Quelled or quenched in leaves the leaping sun,
All felled, felled, are all felled;
    Of a fresh and following folded rank
        Not spared, not one
        That dandled a sandalled
      Shadow that swam or sank
On meadow and river and wind-wandering
    weed-winding bank.

  O if we but knew what we do
      When we delve or hew—
    Hack and rack the growing green!
      Since country is so tender
    To touch, her being so slender,
    That, like this sleek and seeing ball
    But a prick will make no eye at all,
    Where we, even where we mean
      To mend her we end her,
     When we hew or delve:
After-comers cannot guess the beauty been.
  Ten or twelve, only ten or twelve
    Strokes of havoc unselve
      The sweet especial scene,
    Rural scene, a rural scene,
    Sweet especial rural scene.

Duns Scotus's Oxford

Towery city and branchy between towers;
Cuckoo-echoing, bell-swarmèd, lark-charmèd, rook-racked,
    river-rounded;
The dapple-eared lily below thee; that country and town did
Once encounter in, here coped and poisèd powers;

Thou hast a base and brickish skirt there, sours
That neighbour-nature thy grey beauty is grounded
Best in; graceless growth, thou hast confounded
Rural rural keeping—folk, flocks, and flowers.

Yet ah! this air I gather and I release
He lived on; these weeds and waters, these walls are what
He haunted who of all men most sways my spirits to peace;

Of realty the rarest-veinèd unraveller; a not
Rivalled insight, be rival Italy or Greece;
Who fired France for Mary without spot.

Henry Purcell

The poet wishes well to the divine genius of Purcell and praises him that, whereas other musicians have given utterance to the moods of man's mind, he has, beyond that, uttered in notes the very make and species of man as created both in him and in all men generally.

Have fair fallen, O fair, fair have fallen, so dear
To me, so arch-especial a spirit as heaves in Henry Purcell.
An age is now since passed, since parted; with the reversal
Of the outward sentence low lays him, listed to a heresy, here.

Not mood in him nor meaning, proud fire or sacred fear,
Or love or pity or all that sweet notes not his might nursle:
It is the forgèd feature finds me; it is the rehearsal
Of own, of abrupt self there so thrusts on, so throngs the ear.

Let him oh! with his air of angels then lift me, lay me! only I'll
Have an eye to the sakes of him, quaint moonmarks, to his
    pelted plumage under
Wings: so some great stormfowl, whenever he has walked his
    while

The thunder-purple seabeach plumèd purple-of-thunder,
If a wuthering of his palmy snow-pinions scatter a colossal
    smile
Off him, but meaning motion fans fresh our wits with wonder

Peace

When will you ever, Peace, wild wooddove, shy wings shut,
Your round me roaming end, and under be my boughs?
When, when, Peace, will you, Peace? I'll not play hypocrite
To own my heart: I yield you do come sometimes; but
That piecemeal peace is poor peace. What pure peace allows
Alarms of wars, the daunting wars, the death of it?

O surely, reaving Peace, my Lord should leave in lieu
Some good! And so he does leave Patience exquisite,
That plumes to Peace thereafter. And when Peace here does
    house
He comes with work to do, he does not come to coo,
        He comes to brood and sit.

The Bugler's First Communion

A bugler boy from barrack (it is over the hill
There)—boy bugler, born, he tells me, of Irish
        Mother to an English sire (he
Shares their best gifts surely, fall how things will),

This very very day came down to us after a boon he on
My late being there begged of me, overflowing
        Boon in my bestowing,
Came, I say, this day to it—to a First Communion.

Here he knelt then in regimental red.
Forth Christ from cupboard fetched, how fain I of feet
        To his youngster take his treat!
Low-latched in leaf-light housel his too huge godhead.

There! and your sweetest sendings, ah divine,
By it, heavens, befall him! as a heart Christ's darling, dauntless;
        Tongue true, vaunt- and tauntless;
Breathing bloom of a chastity in mansex fine.

Frowning and forefending angel-warder
Squander the hell-rook ranks sally to molest him;
        March, kind comrade, abreast him;
Dress his days to a dexterous and starlight order.

How it does my heart good, visiting at that bleak hill,
When limber liquid youth, that to all I teach
        Yields tender as a pushed peach,
Hies headstrong to its wellbeing of a self-wise self-will!

Then though I should tread tufts of consolation
Days after, so I in a sort deserve to
             And do serve God to serve to
Just such slips of soldiery Christ's royal ration.

Nothing else is like it, no, not all so strains
Us: fresh youth fretted in a bloomfall all portending
             That sweet's sweeter ending;
Realm both Christ is heir to and there reigns.

O now well work that sealing sacred ointment!
O for now charms, arms, what bans off bad
             And locks love ever in a lad!
Let me though see no more of him, and not disappointment

Those sweet hopes quell whose least me quickenings lift,
In scarlet or somewhere of some day seeing
             That brow and bead of being,
An our day's God's own Galahad. Though this child's drift

Seems by a divine doom channelled, nor do I cry
Disaster there; but may he not rankle and roam
             In backwheels though bound home?—
That left to the Lord of the Eucharist, I here lie by;

Recorded only, I have put my lips on pleas
Would brandle adamantine heaven with ride and jar, did
             Prayer go disregarded:
Forward-like, but however, and like favourable heaven heard
      these.

Morning Midday and Evening Sacrifice

The dappled die-away
Cheek and wimpled lip,
The gold-wisp, the airy-grey
Eye, all in fellowship—
This, all this beauty blooming,
This, all this freshness fuming,
Give God while worth consuming.

Both thought and thew now bolder
And told by Nature: Tower;
Head, heart, hand, heel, and shoulder
That beat and breathe in power—
This pride of prime's enjoyment
Take as for tool, not toy meant
And hold at Christ's employment.

The vault and scope and schooling
And mastery in the mind,
In silk-ash kept from cooling,
And ripest under rind—
What life half lifts the latch of,
What hell stalks towards the snatch of,
Your offering, with despatch, of!

Andromeda

Now Time's Andromeda on this rock rude,
With not her either beauty's equal or
Her injury's, looks off by both horns of shore,
Her flower, her piece of being, doomed dragon's food.
    Time past she has been attempted and pursued
By many blows and banes; but now hears roar
A wilder beast from West than all were, more
Rife in her wrongs, more lawless, and more lewd.

    Her Perseus linger and leave her to her extremes?—
Pillowy air he treads a time and hangs
His thoughts on her, forsaken that she seems,
    All while her patience, morselled into pangs,
Mounts; then to alight disarming, no one dreams,
With Gorgon's gear and barebill, thongs and fangs.

The Candle Indoors

Some candle clear burns somewhere I come by.
I muse at how its being puts blissful back
With yellowy moisture mild night's blear-all black,
Or to-fro tender trambeams truckle at the eye.
By that window what task what fingers ply,
I plod wondering, a-wanting, just for lack
Of answer the eagerer a-wanting Jessy or Jack
There   God to aggrandise, God to glorify.—

Come you indoors, come home; your fading fire
Mend first and vital candle in close heart's vault:
You there are master, do your own desire;
What hinders? Are you beam-blind, yet to a fault
In a neighbour deft-handed? are you that liar
And, cast by conscience out, spendsavour salt?

The Handsome Heart

at a Gracious Answer

'But tell me, child, your choice; what shall I buy
You?'—'Father, what you buy me I like best.'
With the sweetest air that said, still plied and pressed,
He swung to his first poised purport of reply.

What the heart is! which, like carriers let fly—·
Doff darkness, homing nature knows the rest—
To its own fine function, wild and self-instressed,
Falls light as ten years long taught how to and why.

Mannerly-hearted! more than handsome face—
Beauty's bearing or muse of mounting vein,
All, in this case, bathed in high hallowing grace . . .

Of heaven what boon to buy you, boy, or gain
Not granted!—Only . . . O on that path you pace
Run all your race, O brace sterner that strain!

At the Wedding March

God with honour hang your head,
Groom, and grace you, bride, your bed
With lissome scions, sweet scions,
Out of hallowed bodies bred.

Each be other's comfort kind:
Deep, deeper than divined,
Divine charity, dear charity,
Fast you ever, fast bind.

Then let the march tread our ears:
I to him turn with tears
Who to wedlock, his wonder wedlock,
Deals triumph and immortal years.

Felix Randal

Felix Randal the farrier, O he is dead then? my duty all ended,
Who have watched his mould of man, big-boned and hardy-
    handsome
Pining, pining, till time when reason rambled in it and some
Fatal four disorders, fleshed there, all contended?

Sickness broke him. Impatient he cursed at first, but mended
Being anointed and all; though a heavenlier heart began some
Months earlier, since I had our sweet reprieve and ransom
Tendered to him. Ah well, God rest him all road ever he
    offended!

This seeing the sick endears them to us, us too it endears.
My tongue had taught thee comfort, touch had quenched thy
    tears,
Thy tears that touched my heart, child, Felix, poor Felix
    Randal;

How far from then forethought of, all thy more boisterous
    years,
When thou at the random grim forge, powerful amidst peers,
Didst fettle for the great grey drayhorse his bright and battering
    sandal!

Brothers

How lovely the elder brother's
Life all laced in the other's,
Love-laced!—what once I well
Witnessed; so fortune fell.
When Shrovetide, two years gone,
Our boys' plays brought on
Part was picked for John,
Young John; then fear, then joy
Ran revel in the elder boy.
Their night was come now; all
Our company thronged the hall;
Henry, by the wall,
Beckoned me beside him:
I came where called, and eyed him
By meanwhiles; making my play
Turn most on tender byplay.
For, wrung all on love's rack,
My lad, and lost in Jack,
Smiled, blushed, and bit his lip;
Or drove, with a diver's dip,
Clutched hands down through clasped knees—
Truth's tokens tricks like these,
Old telltales, with what stress
He hung on the imp's success.
Now the other was brass-bold:
He had no work to hold
His heart up at the strain;
Nay, roguish ran the vein.

Two tedious acts were past;
Jack's call and cue at last;
When Henry, heart-forsook,
Dropped eyes and dared not look.
Eh, how all rung!
Young dog, he did give tongue!
But Harry—in his hands he has flung
His tear-tricked cheeks of flame
For fond love and for shame.

   Ah Nature, framed in fault,
There's comfort then, there's salt;
Nature, bad, base, and blind,
Dearly thou canst be kind;
There dearly then, dearly,
I'll cry thou canst be kind.

Spring and Fall

To a young child

Margaret, are you grieving
Over Goldengrove unleaving?
Leaves, like the things of man, you
With your fresh thoughts care for, can you?
Ah! as the heart grows older
It will come to such sights colder
By and by, nor spare a sigh
Though worlds of wanwood leafmeal lie;
And yet you will weep and know why.
Now no matter, child, the name:
Sorrow's springs are the same.
Nor mouth had, no nor mind, expressed
What heart heard of, ghost guessed:
It is the blight man was born for,
It is Margaret you mourn for.

Inversnaid

This darksome burn, horseback brown,
His rollrock highroad roaring down,
In coop and in comb the fleece of his foam
Flutes and low to the lake falls home.

A windpuff-bonnet of fawn-froth
Turns and twindles over the broth
Of a pool so pitchblack, fell-frowning,
It rounds and rounds Despair to drowning.

Degged with dew, dappled with dew
Are the groins of the braes that the brook treads through,
Wiry heathpacks, flitches of fern,
And the beadbonny ash that sits over the burn.

What would the world be, once bereft
Of wet and of wildness? Let them be left,
O let them be left, wildness and wet;
Long live the weeds and the wilderness yet.

As Kingfishers Catch Fire

As kingfishers catch fire, dragonflies draw flame;
As tumbled over rim in roundy wells
Stones ring; like each tucked string tells, each hung bell's
Bow swung finds tongue to fling out broad its name;
Each mortal thing does one thing and the same:
Deals out that being indoors each one dwells;
Selves—goes itself; *myself* it speaks and spells;
Crying *What I do is me: for that I came.*

I say more: the just man justices;
Keeps grace: that keeps all his goings graces;
Acts in God's eye what in God's eye he is—
Christ—for Christ plays in ten thousand places,
Lovely in limbs, and lovely in eyes not his
To the Father through the features of men's faces.

Ribblesdale

Earth, sweet Earth, sweet landscape, with leaves throng
And louchèd low grass, heaven that dost appeal
To, with no tongue to plead, no heart to feel;
That canst but only be, but dost that long—

Thou canst but be, but that thou well dost; strong
Thy plea with him who dealt, nay does now deal,
Thy lovely dale down thus and thus bids reel
Thy river, and o'er gives all to rack or wrong.

And what is Earth's eye, tongue, or heart else, where
Else, but in dear and dogged man?—Ah, the heir
To his own selfbent so bound, so tied to his turn,
To thriftless reave both our rich round world bare
And none reck of world after, this bids wear
Earth brows of such care, care and dear concern.

The Leaden Echo and the Golden Echo

(Maidens' song from St. Winefred's Well)

THE LEADEN ECHO

How to keep—is there any any, is there none such, nowhere
   known some, bow or brooch or braid or brace, lace, latch
   or catch or key to keep
Back beauty, keep it, beauty, beauty, beauty, . . . from vanishing
   away?
O is there no frowning of these wrinkles, rankèd wrinkles
   deep,
Down? no waving off of these most mournful messengers,
   still messengers, sad and stealing messengers of grey?
No there's none, there's none, O no there's none,
Nor can you long be, what you now are, called fair,
Do what you may do, what, do what you may,
And wisdom is early to despair:
Be beginning; since, no, nothing can be done
To keep at bay
Age and age's evils, hoar hair,
Ruck and wrinkle, drooping, dying, death's worst, winding
   sheets, tombs and worms and tumbling to decay;
So be beginning, be beginning to despair.
O there's none; no no no there's none:
Be beginning to despair, to despair,
Despair, despair, despair, despair.

Spare!
There is one, yes I have one (Hush there!);
Only not within seeing of the sun,
Not within the singeing of the strong sun,
Tall sun's tingeing, or treacherous the tainting of the earth's
    air,
Somewhere elsewhere there is ah well where! one,
One. Yes I can tell such a key, I do know such a place,
Where whatever's prized and passes of us, everything that's
    fresh and fast flying of us, seems to us sweet of us and
    swiftly away with, done away with, undone,
Undone, done with, soon done with, and yet dearly and
    dangerously sweet
Of us, the wimpled-water-dimpled, not-by-morning-matchèd
    face,
The flower of beauty, fleece of beauty, too too apt to, ah! to
    fleet,
Never fleets more, fastened with the tenderest truth
To its own best being and its loveliness of youth: it is an ever-
    lastingness of, O it is an all youth!
Come then, your ways and airs and looks, locks, maiden gear,
    gallantry and gaiety and grace,
Winning ways, airs innocent, maiden manners, sweet looks,
    loose locks, long locks, lovelocks, gaygear, going gallant,
    girlgrace—
Resign them, sign them, seal them, send them, motion them
    with breath,
And with sighs soaring, soaring sighs deliver
Them; beauty-in-the-ghost, deliver it, early now, long before
    death
Give beauty back, beauty, beauty, beauty, back to God,
    beauty's self and beauty's giver.

See; not a hair is, not an eyelash, not the least lash lost; every hair
Is, hair of the head, numbered.
Nay, what we had lighthanded left in surly the mere mould
Will have waked and have waxed and have walked with the
    wind what while we slept,
This side, that side hurling a heavyheaded hundredfold
What while we, while we slumbered.
O then, weary then why should we tread? O why are we so
    haggard at the heart, so care-coiled, care-killed, so fagged,
    so fashed, so cogged, so cumbered,
When the thing we freely forfeit is kept with fonder a care,
Fonder a care kept than we could have kept it, kept
Far with fonder a care (and we, we should have lost it) finer,
    fonder
A care kept.—Where kept? Do but tell us where kept, where.—
Yonder.—What high as that! We follow, now we follow.—
    Yonder, yes yonder, yonder,
Yonder.

The Blessed Virgin compared to the Air we Breathe

Wild air, world-mothering air,
Nestling me everywhere,
That each eyelash or hair
Girdles; goes home betwixt
The fleeciest, frailest-flixed
Snowflake; that's fairly mixed
With, riddles, and is rife
In every least thing's life;
This needful, never spent,
And nursing element;
My more than meat and drink,
My meal at every wink;
This air, which, by life's law,
My lung must draw and draw
Now but to breathe its praise,
Minds me in many ways
Of her who not only
Gave God's infinity
Dwindled to infancy
Welcome in womb and breast,
Birth, milk, and all the rest
But mothers each new grace
That does now reach our race—
Mary Immaculate,
Merely a woman, yet
Whose presence, power is
Great as no goddess's

Was deemèd, dreamèd; who
This one work has to do—
Let all God's glory through,
God's glory which would go
Through her and from her flow
Off, and no way but so.

I say that we are wound
With mercy round and round
As if with air: the same
Is Mary, more by name.
She, wild web, wondrous robe,
Mantles the guilty globe,
Since God has let dispense
Her prayers his providence:
Nay, more than almoner,
The sweet alms' self is her
And men are meant to share
Her life as life does air.
    If I have understood,
She holds high motherhood
Towards all our ghostly good
And plays in grace her part
About man's beating heart,
Laying, like air's fine flood,
The deathdance in his blood;
Yet no part but what will
Be Christ our Saviour still.
Of her flesh he took flesh:
He does take fresh and fresh,
Though much the mystery how,
Not flesh but spirit now
And makes, O marvellous!
New Nazareths in us,

Where she shall yet conceive
Him, morning, noon, and eve;
New Bethlems, and he born
There, evening, noon, and morn—
Bethlem or Nazareth,
Men here may draw like breath
More Christ and baffle death;
Who, born so, comes to be
New self and nobler me
In each one and each one
More makes, when all is done,
Both God's and Mary's Son.

    Again, look overhead
How air is azurèd;
O how! nay do but stand
Where you can lift your hand
Skywards: rich, rich it laps
Round the four fingergaps.
Yet such a sapphire-shot,
Charged, steepèd sky will not
Stain light. Yea, mark you this:
It does no prejudice.
The glass-blue days are those
When every colour glows,
Each shape and shadow shows.
Blue be it: this blue heaven
The seven or seven times seven
Hued sunbeam will transmit
Perfect, not alter it.
Or if there does some soft,
On things aloof, aloft,
Bloom breathe, that one breath more
Earth is the fairer for.
Whereas did air not make

This bath of blue and slake
His fire, the sun would shake,
A blear and blinding ball
With blackness bound, and all
The thick stars round him roll
Flashing like flecks of coal,
Quartz-fret, or sparks of salt,
In grimy vasty vault.

So God was god of old:
A mother came to mould
Those limbs like ours which are
What must make our daystar
Much dearer to mankind;
Whose glory bare would blind
Or less would win man's mind.
Through her we may see him
Made sweeter, not made dim,
And her hand leaves his light
Sifted to suit our sight.

Be thou then, O thou dear
Mother, my atmosphere;
My happier world, wherein
To wend and meet no sin;
Above me, round me lie
Fronting my froward eye
With sweet and scarless sky;
Stir in my ears, speak there
Of God's love, O live air,
Of patience, penance, prayer:
World-mothering air, air wild,
Wound with thee, in thee isled,
Fold home, fast fold thy child.

To what serves Mortal Beauty?

To what serves mortal beauty—dangerous; does set danc-
ing blood—the O-seal-that-so feature, flung prouder form
Than Purcell tune lets tread to? See: it does this: keeps warm
Men's wits to the things that are; what good means—where
    a glance
Master more may than gaze, gaze out of countenance.
Those lovely lads once, wet-fresh windfalls of war's storm,
How then should Gregory, a father, have gleanèd else from
    swarm-
ed Rome? But God to a nation dealt that day's dear chance.
  To man, that needs would worship block or barren stone,
Our law says: Love what are love's worthiest, were all
    known;
World's loveliest—men's selves. Self flashes off frame and
    face.
What do then? how meet beauty? Merely meet it; own,
Home at heart, heaven's sweet gift; then leave, let that alone.
Yea, wish that though, wish all, God's better beauty, grace.

Spelt from Sibyl's Leaves

Earnest, earthless, equal, attuneable, vaulty, voluminous, . . .
    stupendous
Evening strains to be time's vast, womb-of-all, home-of-all,
    hearse-of-all night.
Her fond yellow hornlight wound to the west, her wild
    hollow hoarlight hung to the height
Waste; her earliest stars, earl-stars, stars principal, overbend us,
Fire-featuring heaven. For earth her being has unbound, her
    dapple is at an end, as-
tray or aswarm, all throughther, in throngs; self in self steepèd
    and pashed—quite
Disremembering, dismembering all now. Heart, you round
    me right
With: Our evening is over us; our night whelms, whelms,
    and will end us.
Only the beak-leaved boughs dragonish damask the tool-
    smooth bleak light; black,
Ever so black on it. Our tale, O our oracle! Let life, waned,
    ah let life wind
Off her once skeined stained veined variety upon, all on two
    spools; part, pen, pack
Now her all in two flocks, two folds—black, white; right,
    wrong; reckon but, reck but, mind
But these two; ware of a world where but these two tell, each
    off the other; of a rack
Where, selfwrung, selfstrung, sheathe- and shelterless, thoughts
    against thoughts in groans grind.

The Soldier

Yes. Why do we all, seeing of a soldier, bless him? bless
Our redcoats, our tars? Both these being, the greater part,
But frail clay, nay but foul clay. Here it is: the heart,
Since, proud, it calls the calling manly, gives a guess
That, hopes that, makesbelieve, the men must be no less;
It fancies, feigns, deems, dears the artist after his art;
And fain will find as sterling all as all is smart,
And scarlet wear the spirit of war there express.

Mark Christ our King. He knows war, served this soldiering
    through;
He of all can reeve a rope best. There he bides in bliss
Now, and seeing somewhere some man do all that man can do,
For love he leans forth, needs his neck must fall on, kiss,
And cry 'O Christ-done deed! So God-made-flesh does too:
Were I come o'er again' cries Christ 'it should be this'.

Carrion Comfort

Not, I'll not, carrion comfort, Despair, not feast on thee;
Not untwist—slack they may be—these last strands of man
In me or, most weary, cry *I can no more.* I can;
Can something, hope, wish day come, not choose not to be.
But ah, but O thou terrible, why wouldst thou rude on me
Thy wring-world right foot rock? lay a lionlimb against me?
    scan
With darksome devouring eyes my bruisèd bones? and fan,
O in turns of tempest, me heaped there; me frantic to avoid
    thee and flee?

  Why? That my chaff might fly; my grain lie, sheer and
    clear.
Nay in all that toil, that coil, since (seems) I kissed the rod,
Hand rather, my heart lo! lapped strength, stole joy, would
    laugh, cheer.
Cheer whom though? the hero whose heaven-handling flung
    me, foot trod
Me? or me that fought him? O which one? is it each one?
    That night, that year
Of now done darkness I wretch lay wrestling with (my God!)
    my God.

No Worst, there is None

No worst, there is none. Pitched past pitch of grief,
More pangs will, schooled at forepangs, wilder wring.
Comforter, where, where is your comforting?
Mary, mother of us, where is your relief?
My cries heave, herds-long; huddle in a main, a chief
Woe, world-sorrow; on an age-old anvil wince and sing—
Then lull, then leave off. Fury had shrieked 'No ling-
ering! Let me be fell: force I must be brief'.

O the mind, mind has mountains; cliffs of fall
Frightful, sheer, no-man-fathomed. Hold them cheap
May who ne'er hung there. Nor does long our small
Durance deal with that steep or deep. Here! creep,
Wretch, under a comfort serves in a whirlwind: all
Life death does end and each day dies with sleep.

Tom's Garland

Upon the Unemployed

Tom—garlanded with squat and surly steel
Tom; then Tom's fallowbootfellow piles pick
By him and rips out rockfire homeforth—sturdy Dick;
Tom Heart-at-ease, Tom Navvy: he is all for his meal
Sure, 's bed now. Low be it: lustily he his low lot (feel
That ne'er need hunger, Tom; Tom seldom sick,
Seldomer heartsore; that treads through, prickproof, thick
Thousands of thorns, thoughts) swings though. Commonweal
Little I reck ho! lacklevel in, if all had bread:
What! Country is honour enough in all us—lordly head,
With heaven's lights high hung round, or, mother-ground
That mammocks, mighty foot. But no way sped,
Nor mind nor mainstrength; gold go garlanded
With, perilous, O no; nor yet plod safe shod sound;
               Undenizened, beyond bound
Of earth's glory, earth's ease, all; no one, nowhere,
In wide the world's weal; rare gold, bold steel, bare
               In both; care, but share care—
This, by Despair, bred Hangdog dull; by Rage,
Manwolf, worse; and their packs infest the age.

Harry Ploughman

Hard as hurdle arms, with a broth of goldish flue
Breathed round; the rack of ribs; the scooped flank; lank
Rope-over thigh; knee-nave; and barrelled shank—
                    Head and foot, shoulder and shank—
By a grey eye's heed steered well, one crew, fall to;
Stand at stress. Each limb's barrowy brawn, his thew
That onewhere curded, onewhere sucked or sank—
                    Soared or sank—,
Though as a beechbole firm, finds his, as at a roll-call, rank
And features, in flesh, what deed he each must do—
                    His sinew-service where do.

He leans to it, Harry bends, look. Back, elbow, and liquid
    waist
In him, all quail to the wallowing o' the plough: 's cheek
    crimson; curls
Wag or crossbridle, in a wind lifted, windlaced—
                    See his wind- lilylocks -laced;
Churlsgrace, too, child of Amansstrength, how it hangs or
    hurls
Them—broad in bluff hide his frowning feet lashed! raced
With, along them, cragiron under and cold furls—
                    With-a-fountain's shining-shot furls.

To seem the Stranger lies my Lot

To seem the stranger lies my lot, my life
Among strangers. Father and mother dear,
Brothers and sisters are in Christ not near
And he my peace my parting, sword and strife.
  England, whose honour O all my heart woos, wife
To my creating thought, would neither hear
Me, were I pleading, plead nor do I: I wear-
y of idle a being but by where wars are rife.

  I am in Ireland now; now I am at a third
Remove. Not but in all removes I can
Kind love both give and get. Only what word
Wisest my heart breeds dark heaven's baffling ban
Bars or hell's spell thwarts. This to hoard unheard,
Heard unheeded, leaves me a lonely began.

I Wake and Feel the Fell of Dark

I wake and feel the fell of dark, not day.
What hours, O what black hoürs we have spent
This night! what sights you, heart, saw; ways you went!
And more must, in yet longer light's delay.
　　With witness I speak this. But where I say
Hours I mean years, mean life. And my lament
Is cries countless, cries like dead letters sent
To dearest him that lives alas! away

　I am gall, I am heartburn. God's most deep decree
Bitter would have me taste: my taste was me;
Bones built in me, flesh filled, blood brimmed the curse.
　Selfyeast of spirit a dull dough sours. I see
The lost are like this, and their scourge to be
As I am mine, their sweating selves; but worse.

Patience, Hard Thing!

Patience, hard thing! the hard thing but to pray,
But bid for, Patience is! Patience who asks
Wants war, wants wounds; weary his times, his tasks;
To do without, take tosses, and obey.
  Rare patience roots in these, and, these away,
Nowhere. Natural heart's ivy, Patience masks
Our ruins of wrecked past purpose. There she basks
Purple eyes and seas of liquid leaves all day.

  We hear our hearts grate on themselves: it kills
To bruise them dearer. Yet the rebellious wills
Of us we do bid God bend to him even so.
  And where is he who more and more distils
Delicious kindness?—He is patient. Patience fills
His crisp combs, and that comes those ways we know.

My own Heart let me more have Pity on

My own heart let me more have pity on; let
Me live to my sad self hereafter kind,
Charitable; not live this tormented mind
With this tormented mind tormenting yet.
  I cast for comfort I can no more get
By groping round my comfortless, than blind
Eyes in their dark can day or thirst can find
Thirst's all-in-all in all a world of wet.

Soul, self; come, poor Jackself, I do advise
You, jaded, let be; call off thoughts awhile
Elsewhere; leave comfort root-room; let joy size
At God knows when to God knows what; whose smile
's not wrung, see you; unforeseen times rather—as skies
Betweenpie mountains—lights a lovely mile.

That Nature is a Heraclitean Fire and of the comfort of the Resurrection

Cloud-puffball, torn tufts, tossed pillows flaunt forth, then
    chevy on an air-
built thoroughfare: heaven-roysterers, in gay-gangs they
    throng; they glitter in marches.
Down roughcast, down dazzling whitewash, wherever an elm
    arches,
Shivelights and shadowtackle in long lashes lace, lance, and
    pair.
Delightfully the bright wind boisterous ropes, wrestles, beats
    earth bare
Of yestertempest's creases; in pool and rut peel parches
Squandering ooze to squeezed dough, crust, dust; stanches,
    starches
Squadroned masks and manmarks treadmire toil there
Footfretted in it. Million-fuelèd, nature's bonfire burns on.
But quench her bonniest, dearest to her, her clearest-selvèd
    spark
Man, how fast his firedint, his mark on mind, is gone!
Both are in an unfathomable, all is in an enormous dark
Drowned. O pity and indignation! Manshape, that shone
Sheer off, disseveral, a star, death blots black out; nor mark
         Is any of him at all so stark
But vastness blurs and time beats level. Enough! the Resur-
    rection,
A heart's-clarion! Away grief's gasping, joyless days, de-
    jection.

                    Across my foundering deck shone
A beacon, an eternal beam. Flesh fade, and mortal trash
Fall to the residuary worm; world's wildfire, leave but ash:
                    In a flash, at a trumpet crash,
I am all at once what Christ is, since he was what I am, and
This Jack, joke, poor potsherd, patch, matchwood, immortal
    diamond,
                    Is immortal diamond.

In honour of

St. Alphonsus Rodriguez

Laybrother of the Society of Jesus

Honour is flashed off exploit, so we say;
And those strokes once that gashed flesh or galled shield
Should tongue that time now, trumpet now that field,
And, on the fighter, forge his glorious day.

On Christ they do and on the martyr may;
But be the war within, the brand we wield
Unseen, the heroic breast not outward-steeled,
Earth hears no hurtle then from fiercest fray.

Yet God (that hews mountain and continent,
Earth, all, out; who, with trickling increment,
Veins violets and tall trees makes more and more)
Could crowd career with conquest while there went
Those years and years by of world without event
That in Majorca Alfonso watched the door.

Thou art indeed just, Lord

*Justus quidem tu es, Domine, si disputem tecum: verumtamen
justa loquar ad te: Quare via impiorum prosperatur? &c.*

Thou art indeed just, Lord, if I contend
With thee; but, sir, so what I plead is just.
Why do sinners' ways prosper? and why must
Disappointment all I endeavour end?
   Wert thou my enemy, O thou my friend,
How wouldst thou worse, I wonder, than thou dost
Defeat, thwart me? Oh, the sots and thralls of lust
Do in spare hours more thrive than I that spend,
Sir, life upon thy cause. See, banks and brakes
Now, leavèd how thick! lacèd they are again
With fretty chervil, look, and fresh wind shakes
Them; birds build—but not I build; no, but strain,
Time's eunuch, and not breed one work that wakes.
Mine, O thou lord of life, send my roots rain.

To R. B.

The fine delight that fathers thought; the strong
Spur, live and lancing like the blowpipe flame,
Breathes once and, quenchèd faster than it came,
Leaves yet the mind a mother of immortal song.
Nine months she then, nay years, nine years she long
Within her wears, bears, cares and combs the same:
The widow of an insight lost she lives, with aim
Now known and hand at work now never wrong.

   Sweet fire the sire of muse, my soul needs this;
I want the one rapture of an inspiration.
O then if in my lagging lines you miss
The roll, the rise, the carol, the creation,
My winter world, that scarcely breathes that bliss
Now, yields you, with some sighs, our explanation.

UNFINISHED POEMS

Moonrise

I awoke in the Midsummer not to call night, in the white and
  the walk of the morning:
The moon, dwindled and thinned to the fringe of a finger-
  nail held to the candle,
Or paring of paradisaïcal fruit, lovely in waning but lustreless,
Stepped from the stool, drew back from the barrow, of dark
  Maenefa the mountain;
A cusp still clasped him, a fluke yet fanged him, entangled
  him, not quit utterly.
This was the prized, the desirable sight, unsought, presented so
  easily,
Parted me leaf and leaf, divided me, eyelid and eyelid of
  slumber.

The Woodlark

Teevo cheevo cheevio chee:
O where, what can that be?
Weedio-weedio: there again!
So tiny a trickle of song-strain;
And all round not to be found
For brier, bough, furrow, or green ground
Before or behind or far or at hand
Either left either right
Anywhere in the sunlight.

Well, after all! Ah but hark—
'I am the little woodlark.
The skylark is my cousin and he
Is known to men more than me.
Round a ring, around a ring
And while I sail (must listen) I sing.

To-day the sky is two and two
With white strokes and strains of the blue.
The blue wheat-acre is underneath
And the braided ear breaks out of the sheath,
The ear in milk, lush the sash,
And crush-silk poppies aflash,
The blood-gush blade-gash
Flame-rash rudred
Bud shelling or broad-shed
Tatter-tassel-tangled and dingle-a-danglèd
Dandy-hung dainty head.
And down . . . the furrow dry

Sunspurge and oxeye
And lace-leaved lovely
Foam-tuft fumitory.

I am so very, O so very glad
That I do think there is not to be had
[Anywhere any more joy to be in.
Cheevio:] when the cry within
Says Go on then I go on
Till the longing is less and the good gone,
But down drop, if it says Stop,
To the all-a-leaf of the treetop.
And after that off the bough
[Hover-float to the hedge brow.]

Through the velvety wind V-winged
[Where shake shadow is sun's-eye-ringed]
To the nest's nook I balance and buoy
With a sweet joy of a sweet joy,
Sweet, of a sweet, of a sweet joy
Of a sweet—a sweet—sweet—joy.'

The Times are Nightfall

The times are nightfall, look, their light grows less;
The times are winter, watch, a world undone:
They waste, they wither worse; they as they run
Or bring more or more blazon man's distress.
And I not help. Nor word now of success:
All is from wreck, here, there, to rescue one—
Work which to see scarce so much as begun
Makes welcome death, does dear forgetfulness.

Or what is else? There is your world within.
There rid the dragons, root out there the sin.
Your will is law in that small commonweal . . .

NOTES

EARLY POEMS

1. HEAVEN-HAVEN

Probably written in 1864, when Hopkins was at Oxford and was first attracted by Roman Catholicism. First entitled 'Rest', it shows Pre-Raphaelite influence.

2. THE HABIT OF PERFECTION   1866

This poem was composed in the year of Hopkins' conversion to Roman Catholicism. In it he desires the denial of the bodily senses as an essential step towards perfecting himself for the service of God.

v.1. *whorlèd:* curved and convoluted, like a shell.

v.3. *This ruck and reel . . .:* the crowd and turbulence of the world entangles and distracts ordinary sight.

v.5. *the stir and keep of pride:* the excitement and maintenance of personal vanity.

v.6. *And you unhouse and house the Lord:* you, hands, shall administer the holy sacrament.

v.7. The body shall be clothed in garments fit for the bride of Christ, garments which like the lilies of the field shall not be toiled at or spun.

POEMS, 1876–89

3. THE WRECK OF THE DEUTSCHLAND   1875–76

When Hopkins entered the Jesuit novitiate in 1868, he destroyed his poems and gave up all thoughts of writing poetry as being inconsistent with the profession of a Christian priest. In 1875 the news of how five Franciscan nuns, fleeing from Germany, were drowned at the mouth of the Thames, stirred him so deeply that, at a hint from the Rector of the theological college where he was studying, he composed *The Wreck of the Deutschland*. Not only is this poem the expression of Hopkins' religious convictions, it is also the first attempt in his mature poetic style. He had for some time been meditating upon a new verse form, and it here appears as the first full-length exercise in 'sprung rhythm'. (*See* Introduction.)

Part the First

A meditation upon the greatness of God as felt by one newly converted to Christianity. This is an exceedingly complex and obscure passage, which it seems that Hopkins did not expect to be fully understood. There is no doubt of the urgency and intensity of his intuition of God's power.

A fully extended paraphrase, even if possible, would occupy many pages. The following brief notes are intended as hints towards comprehension.

v.1.   The revelation of God's power almost destroyed me with dread. But once more his grace restores my power of feeling.

v.2.   The struggle and strains of spiritual conversion.

v.3.   *that spell:* during the time of my struggle.

carrier-witted: my heart had the homing instinct of a carrier-pigeon.

v.4.   The life of the body disintegrates like the sand in an hour-glass, but the spirit gains fullness, like the still waters in a well, from the streamlets of God's grace. *voel:* hill.

v.5.   I acknowledge the beauty of the world, since through the senses, and not the understanding only, is God's power intuitively felt (*instressed*, *stressed*).

v.6.   The knowledge of God's saving power, not through bliss alone but also through the pain of Christ's passion, transcends all time.

v.7, 8.   The revelation of God's grace, though first felt in the world at the time of the Crucifixion and Resurrection, must be felt anew by every man for himself in suffering, some finding it bitter, others sweet.

v.9, 10.   May God be adored, and may rebellious man be tamed to his will through suffering and wreck, whether his conversion is sudden and violent like that of St. Paul, or slow, like that of St. Augustine.

Part the Second

Verses 11–16. Description of the wrecking of the 'Deutschland', bound from Germany to America with about 200 refugees, on a sandbank at the mouth of the Thames.

v.11.   Death comes in many forms (*the flange and the rail:* railway disaster); we are apt to forget that we are mortal.

v.12.   *bay:* as in a church.
     reeve: gather.

v.14.   *combs:* ridges.
     Knock: sand-bank on Kentish coast of Thames estuary.
     whorl: propeller.

v.16.   *burl:* confusion, cf. hurly-burly.

v.17, 18, 19.   All despair until a nun arises and calls upon Christ. The thought of her courage inspires the poet to praise and thanksgiving.

v.19.   *sloggering:* buffeting.
     fetch: device (i.e. prayer).

v.20, 21.   The exact meaning is obscure, but the general sense is that this nun was the leader of the five who were exiled from Protestant Germany, where, like Abel and Cain (good and evil sons of the same mother) the Catholic saint, Gertrude, had lived near the birthplace of the 'beast' Luther. God is likened to the hunter Orion, who hunted them out of Germany to show their devotion to him by perishing in the storm.

v.22.   The five nuns are compared to the five stigmata or marks of Christ's wounds, the tokens by which Christians *find* God.

v.23.   *lovescape:* the marks received by St. Francis on becoming a follower of Christ.

v.24.   The Jesuit college of St. Beuno, where Hopkins was studying, was in North Wales.

v.25.   *We are perishing:* see St. Matthew, viii. 25.

v.26.   Does the nun in her distress long for Heaven?

v.27.   No: it is not extreme danger which fathers that asking for ease, but the ordinary wear and tear of daily toil. The burden of her mind would be different during the storm's extremity.

v.28.   The climax of the shipwreck is here directly expressed in the incoherent and broken phrases.

v.29.   Hopkins praises the indomitable courage and steadfastness of the nun, who was bound, as it were, to the stormblast as firmly as the Tarpeian rock (from which criminals were thrown in ancient Rome).

v.30.   The nun is here compared with the Virgin Mary: the date of the disaster was December 7th, eve of the Feast of the Immaculate Conception of the Blessed Virgin.

v.31.   May my heart pity, not only the nun, who has Christ, but also the others who perished.

v.32–35.   The poem concludes with a return to the opening theme, the power and wisdom of God.

v.31.   Adoration of God's power.

> *Yore-flood:* the original Flood of Noah.

v.33.   God's grace has power to redeem all penitent souls.

v.34.   May God's presence be felt again through the love of Christ.

v.35.   May the dead nun help to restore Britain to the true Christian faith.

15. PENMAEN POOL   1876
   Dr. John Pick, in *Gerard Manley Hopkins: Priest and Poet*, calls this poem 'ten facile but unpoetic stanzas for the visitors' book at an inn'.

v.2, 3, 6.   The two mountains, Dyphwys and Cader Idris (Giant's stool) stand on either side of Penmaen Pool, through which flows the river Mawddach.

17. THE SILVER JUBILEE   1876
   This is one of the occasional pieces which Hopkins allowed himself to compose despite his belief that writing poetry was incompatible with the demands of his calling.

18. GOD'S GRANDEUR   1877
   A protest against the materialism of the age; yet despite man's greed and wastefulness, there is hope for the world as long as God continues to brood over it.

l.2.   *foil:* gold leaf or tinsel.

19. THE STARLIGHT NIGHT   1877
   The contemplation of the stars in all their multitude and brilliance suggests a series of ecstatic similes. Then Hopkins asks, 'What is the price of a true love and understanding of the beauty of the universe?' The answer is, 'Prayer, patience, alms, vows'. The stars are the boundaries of Christ's own home.

l.6.   *whitebeam:* small tree with silvery underleaf.

> *abeles:* white poplars.

l.13.   *shocks:* sheaves of corn.

20. SPRING   1877

Spring in the world is compared to the innocent youth of children: Hopkins appeals to Christ to win over their minds for himself before they are corrupted by the world, for it is children who are the first choice of Mary's son and most worth winning.

21. THE LANTERN OUT OF DOORS   1877

l.4. wading: moving.

l.9–10. wind What most I may eye after: however hard I try to follow with my eye their winding path.

22. THE SEA AND THE SKYLARK   1877

Hopkins was at this time obsessed by the corruption of man compared with the primal innocence of nature.

l.6–7. rash-fresh re-winded . . .: This was the subject of a lengthy explanation by Hopkins in a letter to Bridges. The meaning is: (I hear) his headlong and exciting song (score means the printed notes in music) whirl (through the air), like a skein of new silk running off the reel (winch) on which it has been re-wound.

l.10. How ring right out; how the sea and the skylark out-ring (as a coin or a bell made of pure metal out-rings a counterfeit).

l.12. cheer: comely appearance.

23. THE WINDHOVER   1877

In 1879 Hopkins described this poem as 'the best thing I ever wrote'. The windhover (*o* short as in 'proverb') or kestrel appears to Hopkins as the symbol of Christ Himself. The following is a rough paraphrase:

'This morning I caught sight of morning's darling, prince of day-light's kingdom, the falcon drawn against the dappled dawn, riding upon the level steady air which rolled beneath him, and striding aloft—I saw how he seemed in his ecstasy to hang upon his rippling wing, like one pulling on a rein! Then off he flew like the heel of a skate sweeping round a bow-shaped curve: his plunging and gliding seemed to push back the wind. My heart, unseen, responded to his achievement and mastery. At this point (where the falcon turns) your animal beauty, your valour, and your action (Hopkins is now apostrophising both the falcon and Christ) seemed to bend or buckle, O air and pride and plume! and the fiery red dawnlight which then is reflected from you, O my prince, is a billion times lovelier than

85

ever! And no wonder, for the mere plodding of a plough-horse makes a ploughshare gleam as it cuts the furrow; and the cold grey-blue embers of a dying fire, O beloved one, as they fall, split open and reveal a gash of red-hot gold.'

24. PIED BEAUTY   1877
l.2. *brinded:* brindled, streaked.

25. HURRAHING IN HARVEST   1877
Hopkins here expresses the idea that the beauty of the world is incomprehensible except as a manifestation of God's presence.
l.1. *barbarous:* wild, perhaps also with suggestions of bearded.
l.2–4. The unity of earth and sky is suggested by the comparison of clouds to drifts of meal or flour, recalling the corn-stooks on the ground.
l.6. *glean:* that is, gather knowledge of Christ as gleaners gather corn after the harvest.
l.7–8. *And, eyes, heart, what looks . . .:* Then what living person ever gave to the eyes and heart of a lover more real and rapturous replies than the clouds gave me as I looked to them for knowledge of Christ?

26. THE CAGED SKYLARK   1877
The body is a prison for the soul only out of its true relation with man as a whole—that is, when it is in pain through excessive drudgery or excessive indulgence of the senses. Just as the skylark has a true resting-place in its own 'free fells', so the soul of man has its true resting-place in a body 'uncumbered' by sin or pain. The Christianity in which Hopkins believed did not deny the body or the senses; it regarded the soul as spiritually higher, but the body also had its true function as the house of the soul. The though in this sonnet is subtler and more difficultt than at first appears.
l.1. *scanted:* half-starved.
l.5. A piece of turf was sometimes placed inside a birdcage.
l.13–14. 'A meadow no more feels the pressure, the discomfort, of the rainbow which rests on it than the new man feels his body.' (Dr. J. Pick.)

27. IN THE VALLEY OF THE ELWY   1877
In a letter (quoted by W. H. Gardner) Hopkins says of this sonnet: 'The kind people of the sonnet were the Watsons of Shooter's Hill,

nothing to do with the Elwy. . . . The frame of the sonnet is a rule of three sum *wrong*, thus: As the sweet smell to those kind people so the Welsh landscape is NOT to the Welsh; and then the author and principle of all four terms is asked to bring the sum right.'

28. THE LOSS OF THE EURYDICE   1878
v.2.   *forefalls:* seaward slopes (cf. foreshore).
v.8.   The places mentioned are in the Isle of Wight.
v.12.   *wrapped in Cheer's death:* having a look of death-like gloom.
v.13.   *Right, rude of feature . . .:* He thought he heard Right (i.e. Justice) with her rude features say, 'You are the ship's commander and you must go down with her'.
v.14.   In a letter to Bridges, Hopkins explained that he did not here accuse the captain of cowardice, but that in times of great stress *even* unconscientious men sometimes made the right choice.
v.17.   *rivelling:* i.e. causing him to screw up his face in an effort to see,
v.23.   This stanza refers to acts of vandalism against Catholic shrines at the time of the Reformation ('bygones').
v.24-25.   Hopkins here regrets the lapse of the British people from their former adherence to the Church of Rome.
v.26.   In Catholic times one observing the stars would have said that the Milky Way pointed to the shrine of Walsingham, as was once believed in the Isle of Wight.

34. THE MAY MAGNIFICAT   1878
   This is an occasional piece composed to be hung with others, anonymously, before the statue of the Virgin Mary at Stonyhurst during May. Dr. John Pick says: 'Obviously it is not in his characteristic manner, for it was an attempt to appeal to the popular taste and Hopkins admitted that in such writing he usually felt himself "to come short".' Writing to Bridges, Hopkins said, 'A Maypiece in which I see little good but the freedom of the rhythm.'
v.2.   *Candlemas:* Feast of the Purification of the Virgin Mary, February 2nd.
         Lady Day: Feast of the Annunciation, March 25th.
v.6.   *bugle:* kind of blue flower (*ajuga reptans*).
v.11.   *azuring-over greybell:* i.e. the greyish buds of the bluebell turning blue as they open.

37. DUNS SCOTUS'S OXFORD   1879

Here Hopkins writes of the Oxford he loved, contrasting its modern development with its medieval beauty. He was greatly influenced in his thought by the medieval theologian Johannes Duns Scotus, who is supposed to have lectured in Oxford about the year 1300.

*l.*3-4.   *that country . . . powers:* in the city where once country and town met, intellectual forces also contended in argument and controversy.

*l.*12.   *Of realty the rarest-veinèd unraveller:* the subtlest of all enquirers into the nature of reality.

*l.*14.   *Who fired France for Mary without spot:* it is believed that Duns Scotus defended the dogma of the Immaculate Conception in Paris.

38. HENRY PURCELL   1879

An obscure tribute to a great musician whom Hopkins admired because his music seemed to express, not only the moods and passions of men, like the music of others, but his own soul and the soul of mankind. Hopkins goes some way to explain his meaning in the argument at the head of the poem.

*l.*1-4.   Hopkins explains this as follows: 'May Purcell have died a good death . . . so that the heavy condemnation under which he outwardly lay for being out of the true Church may in consequence of his good intentions have been reversed.'

*l.*9-14.   In a letter to Bridges, Hopkins says: 'The sestet . . . is not so clearly worked out as I could wish. The thought is that as the seabird opening his wings with a whiff of wind in your face means the whirr of the motion but also unaware gives you a whiff of knowledge about his plumage, the marking of which stamps his species, that he does not mean, so Purcell, seemingly intent only on the thought or feeling he is to express or call out, incidentally lets you remark the individualising marks of his own genius.'

*l.*10.   *sakes:* Hopkins explains this as meaning Purcell's individual marks of genius.

   moonmarks: 'Crescent-shaped markings on the quill-feathers, either in the colouring of the feather or made by the overlapping of one on another.' (Hopkins, Letter to Bridges.)

*l.*13.   *wuthering:* 'A Northcountry word for the noise and rush of wind.' (Hopkins, Letter to Bridges.)

39. PEACE   1879

l.2.   Your round me roaming end: finish circling round me.

l.4.   To own my heart: to my own heart.

l.7.   reaving: i.e. depriving me of.

l.9.   plumes to: i.e. grows feathers in time and becomes the fully
fledged dove of peace.

40. THE BUGLER'S FIRST COMMUNION   1879

v.3.   housel: consecrated wafer (too light to contain—*latch*—Christ's
divinity).

v.5.   Squander the hell-rook ranks sally: scatter the birds of ill-omen
which sally.

        Dress his days . . .: make the rest of his days like a smartly dressed
and fortunate company of soldiers. (Note the military metaphor here
and elsewhere in this poem.)

v.8.   not all so strains Us: nothing else obliges us (to hope for and
sympathise with it as the promise of youth).

v.9.   O for now charms . . .: O for charms and arms and whatever drives
away evil and keeps the love of God in a boy!

v.10.   An our day's . . .: if he is the pattern of stainless knighthood to our
day and to God.

v.11.   but may he not rankle and roam In backwheels though bound home?:
but may he not slip and wander backwards though Heaven-bound?

42. MORNING MIDDAY AND EVENING SACRIFICE   1879

    Three stages in the growth of body and mind as offered in sacrifice
to God.

v.1.   wimpled: curving, rippling.

        fuming: passing away like smoke.

v.3.   in silk-ash: the grey or silver hair of the old man is compared to
the silky grey ash covering wood-embers which still glow.

        Your offering, with despatch, of! Hopkins explains this as a command,
like 'Your money or your life!' i.e. 'Come, your offer of all this (the
matured mind) and without delay either!'

43. ANDROMEDA   1879

    Here Hopkins represents the Catholic Church as Andromeda on the
rock (that of St. Peter), a prey to various enemies from the west, i.e.
the intellectual currents of the nineteenth century, materialism, etc. until

Christ's second coming as her champion in the form of Perseus, who will disarm and destroy her enemies.

44. THE CANDLE INDOORS 1879

l.4.   *Or to-fro tender trambeams . . .:* delicate parallel rays which waver at the least motion of the eyelids.

l.9–14.   Here Hopkins turns upon himself and rebukes himself for hoping that the unknown Jessy or Jack at the candle-lit window might be a better Christian; he asks himself whether he is not the hypocrite referred to in the Sermon on the Mount, and urges himself to let his light shine before men, and to cast the beam out of his own eye before observing the mote in his neighbour's.

45. THE HANDSOME HEART 1879

This sonnet is based on the story of an offer of money by Father Hopkins to a boy who had helped him: the boy refused money and was finally induced to accept a book.

The first part of the sonnet makes the point that, rightly taught, the heart knows naturally how to do what is right, i.e. God's will, 'doffing darkness' (putting sin aside). In the latter part, Hopkins breaks off in his admiration of the boy's 'mannerly heart' to ask himself what prayer he shall make for him, and in conclusion prays that the boy may be given grace to pursue the right path through life's hardships.

46. AT THE WEDDING MARCH 1879

47. FELIX RANDAL 1880

This is the first of Hopkins' Liverpool poems, and introduces Lancashire dialect expressions—*and all* (line 6), *all road ever* (8), i.e. in whatever way; *fettle* (14), put in order.

l.13.   *random:* W. H. Gardner points out that this is an architectural term meaning 'built of stones of irregular shapes and sizes'. It probably also has the significance of 'thoughtless, unthinking', in contrast to the blacksmith's later mood.

48. BROTHERS 1880

50. SPRING AND FALL 1880

This poem expresses the idea of the 'sad mortality' of man and nature alike. The child that weeps because of the golden leaves falling in

autumn really mourns, though she does not yet know it, her own
mortality.

51.   INVERSNAID   1881
l.1.   *In coop and in comb:* in hollows and crests.
l.2.   *twindles:* a coinage, probably with sense of twining and dwindling.
l.3.   *Degged:* sprinkled (Northern dialect).

52.   AS KINGFISHERS CATCH FIRE   No title or date.
   In this sonnet Hopkins expresses in his own way a religious idea
derived partly from the medieval theologian, Duns Scotus. Everything
expresses its own nature and exists for that purpose alone. Not only
natural objects and creatures, but also men fulfil themselves in the eye
of God, and exist to express God through their own nature.
l.3.   *tucked:* touched.
l.7.   *Selves:* fulfils itself.

53.   RIBBLESDALE   1882
   A poem against the spoliation of nature for the sake of man's profit
and self-interest. Nature has no guardian but man, and such beauty as
that of Ribblesdale (Lancashire) pleads with man to show concern for
its preservation.
l.1.   *throng:* adjective—dense, thick (dialect).
l.2.   *louchèd:* 'is a coinage of mine, and is to mean much the same as
slouched, slouching ' (Letter by Hopkins to Dixon).
l.11.   *selfbent:* self-will, self-interest.
l.12.   *reave:* strip.

54.   THE LEADEN ECHO AND THE GOLDEN ECHO   1882
   St. Winifred's Well was a verse drama of which Hopkins wrote only
fragments. Of this song he wrote some years later, 'I never did anything
more musical', and it is clear that he was here trying to produce some of
the effects of music, an art in which he had a life-long and more than
casual interest.
l.4.   *Down:* goes with frowning. Frowning down means 'discourage-
ment by rebuke'.
l.42.   *fashed:* troubled.
         cogged: deceived.

57. THE BLESSED VIRGIN COMPARED TO THE AIR WE BREATHE   1883

l.5.   flixed: furred.

l.40.   Since God has let dispense Her prayers his providence: i.e. Since God
has let her prayers dispense his providence (Mary being the mediator
between God and men). A good example of Hopkins' fluid word-order.

l.103–106.   Christ, being born of Mary in human form, is dearer to us.

l.108–109.   God's glory, revealed directly and not through Christ,
would blind men or be less winning.

61. TO WHAT SERVES MORTAL BEAUTY?   1885

   A highly complex intellectual argument in which is compressed
much of Hopkins' belief about the nature and purpose of beauty. It is,
he says, 'dangerous', i.e. as a distraction from the spiritual life, yet it has
its true purpose in the creator's scheme; for a sudden revelation of mortal
beauty gives insight into the divine nature of man. Thus Pope Gregory,
about the year 600, seeing some fair-haired, blue-eyed Briton slaves in
Rome, uttered his famous pun, 'Non Angli sed angeli', and sent
Augustine as the first Christian missionary to Britain. Let the
observer contemplate beauty, Hopkins concludes, but not desire to
possess it.

l.2.   the O-seal-that-so feature: the physical or facial feature which causes
the artist to exclaim at its beauty, wishing that it could be 'sealed',
perpetuated, for ever.

62. SPELT FROM SIBYL'S LEAVES   1885

   The first of Hopkins' few final poems written in Dublin—sombre,
self-torturing and bitter. He was undergoing what an early Christian
mystic called 'the dark night of the soul', when he felt that his God,
for whom he had given up everything, had deserted him. He gives this
poem a classical title as if to imply that what it says came from the
writings of some prophetess earlier, more mysterious and more remote
than Christianity itself. As evening darkens into night, he feels that an
immense night of self-examination is upon him, a night of self-torturing
agony and introspection. In such a night, all the 'dapple' of daytime—
all the sensuous delight in appearances, as well as all the half-truths and
ambiguities with which we surround ourselves in life—are swallowed
up, and nothing but absolute right and wrong remains—everything is
black or white, and the final judgement is upon him.

l.1.   *attuneable:* harmonious.
l.6.   *throughther:* through one another, i.e. mixed up.
          pashed: beaten.
l.7.   *Disremembering:* in using this Irishism for 'forgetting', Hopkins shows his sensitivity to local dialect expressions. Compare his use of Lancashire words in *Felix Randal*.
          round: warn.
l.11.   *part, pen, pack now her all . . .:* i.e. let life divide everything it contained into two flocks, black and white.

63.   THE SOLDIER   1885

   We all bless and love a soldier or a sailor because his is a noble calling, and we like to believe that the calling has ennobled the man, just as we hold an artist dear on account of his art. Christ himself was a soldier; he knew the art of seamanship: when he sees a deed nobly done, he loves and praises the doer: we, formed in Christ's image, do likewise. If Christ were to come again, it would be in the likeness of a brave man.

64.   CARRION COMFORT   1885

   Hopkins described this sonnet as having been 'written in blood'. The title was added by Bridges. It expresses the sense of abandonment by the God for whom he had sacrificed everything, and the resolution not to give way to despair and suicide. In lines 5–8 he imagines God as a terrible lion crushing him to earth under his foot, while he—the writer—struggles hopelessly to escape. What, he goes on to ask, is the purpose of this torture? It is that all earthly impurity shall be cast away like chaff and the spirit emerge pure and unencumbered. Does the comfort he derived from kissing the rod—that is, from rejoicing in the tribulation God imposed—please God or himself? In the last two lines he refers to the 'dark night of the soul' in which he made his bitter spiritual self-examination.

65.   NO WORST, THERE IS NONE   ?1885–1887
   A direct cry from the heart, expressing the extreme of desolation.
l.5–6.   My cries of agony follow one another like cattle in a herd, huddling together under one enormous sorrow (cf. German. *Weltschmerz*).

l.8. *force:* perforce.

l.10–11. *Hold them cheap May who ne'er hung there:* let him make light of them (i.e. the minds mountains of terror from which the sufferer plunges into abysses of despair) who never experienced them.

l.12–14. In the whirlwind of spiritual torment, let the poor soul seek comfort in the knowledge that the day's agony dies with the day and all agony ends with death. 'all Life . . .' etc., refers back to 'Here!'

66. TOM'S GARLAND   1887

Of this sonnet, Hopkins wrote to Bridges: 'It means then that, as St. Paul and Plato and Hobbes and everybody says, the commonwealth or well-ordered human society is like one man; a body with many members and each its function; some higher, some lower, but all honourable, from the honour which belongs to the whole. The head is the sovereign, who has no superior but God and from heaven receives his or her authority: we must then imagine this head as bare (see St. Paul much on this) and covered, so to say, only with the sun and stars, of which the crown is a symbol, which is an ornament but not a covering; it has an enormous hat or skull-cap, the vault of heaven. The foot is the day-labourer, and this is armed with hobnail boots, because it has to wear and be worn by the ground; which again is symbolical; for it is navvies or day-labourers who, on the great scale or in gangs and millions, mainly trench, tunnel, blast, and in other ways disfigure, 'mammock' the earth and, on a small scale, singly, and superficially stamp it with their footprints. And the 'garlands' of nails they wear are therefore the visible badge of the place they fill, the lowest in the commonwealth. But this place still shares the common honour, and if it wants one advantage, glory or public fame, makes up for it by another, ease of mind, absence of care; and these things are symbolised by the gold and the iron garlands (O, once explained, how clear it all is!). Therefore the scene of the poem is laid at evening, when they are giving over work and one after another pile their picks, with which they earn their living, and swing off home, knocking sparks out of mother earth not now by labour and of choice but by the mere footing, being strongshod and making no hardship of hardness, taking all easy. And so to supper and bed. Here comes a violent but effective hyperbaton or suspension, in which the action of the mind mimics that of the labourer—surveys his lot, low but free from care; then by a sudden strong act throws it over the shoulder or tosses it away as a light matter.

94

The witnessing of which lightheartedness makes me indignant with the fools of Radical Levellers. But presently I remember that this is all very well for those who are in, however low in, the Commonwealth and share in any way the common weal; but that the curse of our times is that many do not share it, that they are outcasts from it and have neither security nor splendour; that they share care with the high and obscurity with the low, but wealth or comfort with neither. And this state of things, I say, is the origin of Loafers, Tramps, Cornerboys, Roughs, Socialists and other pests of society. And I think that it is a very pregnant sonnet, and in point of execution very highly wrought, too much so, I am afraid. . . .'

67. HARRY PLOUGHMAN 1887

Hopkins thought highly of this sonnet, and insisted that it was written to be recited, not read silently. He described the poem as 'a direct picture of a ploughman, without afterthought'. Nevertheless, in lines 6–11 ('Each limb's . . . sinew-service where do') Hopkins expresses the idea that the beauty of the ploughman at work depends on the appropriateness of every movement and appearance, and in the co-ordination of eye, limb and muscle.

(This sonnet appears to have more than the usual 14 lines, but the extra 5 half-lines are additions—Hopkins called them 'burden-lines'— intended to be recited by a chorus.)

l.1. flue: fluff or down.
l.3. knee-nave: kneecap.
l.6. barrowy: mounded, suggesting hillocks.
l.7. curded: knotted, thickened.
l.13. 's cheek: his cheek.
l.15. See his wind- lilylocks -laced: see how his locks, fair as lilies, are crossed or plaited by the wind.
l.18. cragiron under and cold furls: presumably the ploughshare and the earth sliced up by it at the side of the furrow.

68. TO SEEM THE STRANGER LIES MY LOT ?1885

No title or date. This and the three following sonnets are probably among those referred to in a letter to Bridges in which Hopkins says, 'Four of these came like inspirations unbidden and against my will. And in the life I lead now, which is one of a continually jaded and harassed mind, if in any leisure I try to do anything I make no way—nor with my work, alas! but so it must be.'

Here Hopkins expresses his sense of isolation from those he loves, who are not Catholics, and from the country of his birth, whose policy in Ireland he did not approve of, and from those who should be reading and understanding his poetry. In the concluding lines he feels that both Heaven and Hell prevent his free utterance, and that to have to hoard his words unheeded leaves him in the loneliness of one who only made a beginning.

69. I WAKE AND FEEL THE FELL OF DARK   ?1885
     No title or date. See first paragraph of preceding note.
     Here Hopkins expresses most powerfully and painfully a bitter self-hatred. He wakes at night and feels the darkness of this emotion suffocating him like the hide of an animal. It is, he says, the will of God that he (Hopkins) must leave a bitter taste in his own mouth. His bones, flesh and blood, as if accursed, are like heavy dough soured by his own sour spirit.
l.1.   *fell:* hide.
l.7.   *dead letters:* undeliverable letters (at post office). It was one of the bitterest features of Hopkins' spiritual agony of this period that he felt as if Christ were completely withdrawn from him.

70. PATIENCE, HARD THING!   ?1885
     No title or date. See first paragraph of note to *To seem the Stranger lies my Lot.*
l.2–3.   *Patience who asks Wants war, wants wounds:* he who asks for patience really desires strife and action.
l.6–14.   The simile of patience as the ivy which covers our past failures gives place to that of God as the patient bee filling his honey-combs with the sweetness he has distilled from the flowers of man's patience.
l.10.   *dearer:* worse. (Cf. Shakespeare: 'my dearest foe'.)

71. MY OWN HEART LET ME MORE HAVE PITY ON   ?1885
     No title or date. See first paragraph of note to *To seem the Stranger lies my Lot.*
     Hopkins here urges himself to cease from mental self-torture and allow his heart time and leisure for consolation.

l.7. *or thirst . . .:* this recalls the verse in *The Ancient Mariner* beginning ''Water, water everywhere'.

l.9. *Jackself:* workaday self.

l.11. *let joy size . . .:* let joy increase in its own good time and place.

l.11–14. *whose smile's not wrung . . .:* joy's smile cannot be forced, but rather at unexpected moments lights up a whole mile of countryside, like a shaft of sunlight dappling the sky between mountains. (*Betweenpie* is a verb coined by Hopkins, meaning to variegate or dapple.)

72. THAT NATURE IS A HERACLITEAN FIRE   1888

Heraclitus, a Greek philosopher who flourished about 500 B.C., taught that all nature is in a state of flux or change, since everything is formed out of the element fire. Hopkins elaborates this idea, pointing out how all man's work and being are obliterated as the weather obliterates the traces of his 'treadmire toil'. How pitiful, he says, that man, the crown of creation, should be destined for such utter darkness! Then comes the thought of Christ's resurrection, and of the resurrection of man's soul in the likeness of Christ; at the sound of the last trumpet, the commonest man becomes precious and indestructible, 'immortal diamond'.

l.4. *Shivelights:* slices of light.

l.6. *rutpeel:* peelings of dried mud from the edges of ruts.

l.11. *firedint:* the mark or impression made by man on the universal element, fire—i.e., man's peculiar physical nature.

l.18. *Across my foundering deck:* note how in referring to states of mental and spiritual conflict Hopkins turns to the idea of shipwreck, as in *The Deutschland* and *The Eurydice*.

l.23. *This Jack, joke, poor potsherd, patch, matchwood:* this common man, this comic piece of broken pottery, this fool, this worthless stick of firewood.

74. IN HONOUR OF ST. ALPHONSUS RODRIGUEZ   1888

This sonnet was written in honour of a Catholic Saint who for forty years acted as hall-porter in the Jesuit college in Palma, Majorca, and was said to be much troubled by evil spirits. Like *Patience, Hard Thing!* this sonnet praises the virtue of inner fortitude. In spite of the Saint's outwardly uneventful forty years, God (patient creator of natural forms) crowded his inner life with victory over evil spirits.

This sonnet expresses a sense of bitter rebellion against God, who allows sinners to prosper while he, the servant of God, writhes beneath the consciousness of failure, frustration and creative barrenness. The Latin quotation at the head of the poem is from Chapter 12 of the Book of Jeremiah; in the Authorised Version it runs:

> 'Righteous art thou, O Lord, when I plead with thee; yet let me talk with thee of thy judgments: Wherefore doth the way of the wicked prosper? wherefore are all they happy that deal very treacherously? Thou hast planted them, yea, they have taken root: they grow, yea, they bring forth fruit: thou art near in their mouth, and far from their reins.'

In its expression of the theme of creative barrenness, Coleridge's sonnet, *Work without Hope* offers a remarkable parallel.

> All Nature seems at work. Slugs leave their lair—
> The bees are stirring—birds are on the wing—
> And Winter slumbering in the open air,
> Wears on his smiling face a dream of Spring!
> And I the while, the sole unbusy thing,
> Nor honey make nor pair, nor build, nor sing.

*l.*11. *fretty chervil:* cow-parsley whose leaves are like lace or fretwork.

Addressed to Bridges, this sonnet gives an account of the process of poetic creation, which is compared to the conception and birth of a child. The original moment of inspiration, compared to a spur or the fierce flame of a blowpipe, is the 'sire' or father; the mind, or the poet's Muse, is the mother. 'Widowed' after the expiration of the original impulse, she labours to produce in due time the 'immortal song'. If, Hopkins goes on, his friend misses in his poems the note of passionate spontaneity ('the roll, the rise, the carol, the creation'), the explanation is afforded by 'my winter world'—that is, the time of spiritual barrenness through which he was passing.

This was Hopkins' last poem. It is doubtful if any great poet has ended his poetic life on a note of deeper hopelessness and desolation.

UNFINISHED POEMS

l.5. A cusp still clasped him, a fluke yet fanged him: the picture is of one point of the moon appearing still to spear or pierce the top of the mountain. *Cusp* and *fluke* are both words for point or barb.

78. THE WOODLARK   1876
   Hopkins left one MS. draft of this uncompleted poem. When it was printed in *The Month* in 1936, Father Geoffrey Bliss, S.J. supplied the lines given in square brackets in order that a beautiful poem should not be spoilt by gaps in the sense.

80. THE TIMES ARE NIGHTFALL   undated
   For the thought in this unfinished sonnet, compare *Spelt from Sibyl's Leaves*. Hopkins expresses once more the sense of frustration and despair at being unable to improve the world's lot, and says that the only alternative is to purify the inner world of the soul.
l.3–4. they as they run . . .: as these evil times go on, they either increase man's distress or increasingly advertise it.

APPENDIX

The following is a reprint of *Spelt from Sibyl's Leaves* as it appears in the standard editions, with Bridges' selection from the accents in Hopkins' two manuscripts.

Earnest, earthless, equal, attuneable, ǀ vaulty, voluminous, . . . stupendous

Evening strains to be tíme's vást, ǀ womb-of-all, home-of-all, hearse-of-all night.

Her fond yellow hornlight wound to the west, ǀ her wild hollow hoarlight hung to the height

Waste; her earliest stars, earl-stars, ǀ stárs principal, overbend us,

Fíre-féaturing heaven. For earth ǀ her being has unbound, her dapple is at an end, as-

tray or aswarm, all throughther, in throngs; ǀ self ín self steepèd and páshed—qúite

Disremembering, dísmémbering ǀ áll now. Heart, you round me right

With: Óur évening is over us; óur night ǀ whélms, whélms, ánd will end us.

Only the beak-leaved boughs dragonish ǀ damask the tool-smooth bleak light; black,

Ever so black on it. Óur tale, O óur oracle! ǀ Lét life, wáned, ah lét life wind

Off hér once skéined stained véined varíety ǀ upon, áll on twó spools; párt, pen, páck

Now her áll in twó flocks, twó folds—black, white; ǀ right, wrong; reckon but, reck but, mind

But thése two; wáre of a wórld where bút these ǀ twó tell, each off the óther; of a rack

Where, selfwrung, selfstrung, sheathe- and shelterless, ǀ thóughts agaínst thoughts ín groans grínd.

INDEX OF TITLES AND FIRST LINES